ANGELIC GUIDANCE HEALING

Copyright © 2025 Maureen Hollmeyer

All rights reserved. This book or any portion may not be reproduced, transmitted, or stored in any manner without written permission of the author.

Disclaimer: The information in this book is provided for entertainment purposes only. All content is based on the author's opinion and does not constitute any health, medical, financial, or legal advice. The ideas, suggestions, and procedures provided in this book are not intended to be a substitute for seeking professional guidance. It is not intended to diagnose, treat, cure, or prevent any condition or disease. Seek advice from your licensed healthcare provider for any conditions or concerns you have prior to reading and completing any of the techniques described in this book. The author makes no guarantee of financial or health-related results obtained by using this book. The author assumes no responsibility and shall not be held liable or responsible for any direct or indirect losses – including, but not limited to, illness, injury, damage, liability, death, or financial loss – allegedly arising from any suggestion, use, or implementation of any information contained in this book.

Images created using Canva.

Ebook ISBN: 979-8-9868370-7-9
Paperback ISBN: 979-8-9868370-8-6

ANGELIC GUIDANCE HEALING

Break Free From Trauma & Create Healthy Connections For You & Your Pet

MAUREEN HOLLMEYER, HTACP

CONTENTS

Dedication i
Acknowledgements iii
Introduction 1
Chapter 1: What is Trauma? 7
Chapter 2: Why Empaths, Lightworkers & Other Healing Professionals? . 23
Chapter 3: Angelic Assistance 34
Chapter 4: Everything Is Energy – 8 Ways to Use Energy for Healing 51
Chapter 5: 10 Spiritual Tools for Trauma Healing 69
Chapter 6: Numerology, Astrology, Genogram, and Chakra Charts 89
Chapter 7: How Do I Know If I'm Healed? 108
What is the Meaning of Life? 127
Footnotes & Resources 135
About the Author 139

DEDICATION

I'm dedicating this book to my husband, Jon, who has loved me unconditionally for over twenty years. Thank you for letting me be unapologetically myself and making another dream come true! You are the wind beneath my wings!

ACKNOWLEDGEMENTS

I want to extend a big thank you to my publisher, Jaclyn Johnston, who is the CEO of Manifest It!® I appreciate you and all of your patience, support, and motivation while helping me publish my book in under 10 weeks! Also, thank you for making it easy for me to decide which publisher I should choose; my angels couldn't have made it any clearer with MANIFEST IT!® Thank you to my editor, Melis, who helped me combine both aspects of my business, people, and pets!

INTRODUCTION

How stressful is your life? Does it feel like you just can't catch a break? Are you living in survival mode, running like a hamster in a wheel to the future you dream of, but unable to move forward?

You struggle to move even the slightest bit while watching others succeed easily. It can seem unfair, like the whole world is against you. But what if it's not some supernatural force holding you back, but the way you view your own life experiences? What if that meant you had the power to turn your life around right here and now?

Everyone experiences trauma of some sort. Trauma is an event that causes you distress mentally, emotionally, physically, and spiritually. This event can be a one-time occurrence, like witnessing a tragic accident or death, or it can be a series of ongoing events, such as child abuse or domestic violence.

What most people don't understand is that trauma can affect you for your entire lifetime if you don't get help.

The individual may think, "I'm glad that the situation is over with," unbeknownst to them, they already developed side effects (especially in the case of child abuse). Child abuse has the most complications with long-term effects since it occurs during the most critical stages of psychological development.

Humans and animals go through similar experiences, such as losing a sibling, abandonment, and feeling scared, hurt, or lost. On the positive side, they both experience joy, happiness, love, and gratitude.

As you can see, animals share many similarities with humans. They share the same needs, emotions, and behaviors. Most of all, many shelter pets are traumatized and need special TLC to heal their behaviors as a result.

Humans connect with animals in ways beyond words. It's as if the animal is the other half of their soul, and I remind clients that their pet is a part of their soul family. Animals don't need to be told that their human needs help, since they can sense it, feel it, and see it in us. Horses know what kind of mood we're in before we set foot into their barn.

Some people enjoy the simple act of caring for an animal, which helps them on their own healing journey. When humans care for an animal, the animal returns the favor through emotions or behaviors to console their owner.

I trained a golden retriever in basic commands that was explicitly purchased for a couple's handicapped son, and over eight weeks, I got to watch their friendship develop. The dog was his companion, bringing a great deal of excitement to his life, and his laughter brought so much joy to the household.

Police dogs are excellent safeguards for their partners and are treated as another member of the police force. They keep each other safe during active duty, and they have a telepathic understanding of what's allowed and what isn't. The most heart-wrenching event to witness is when the dog remains by the funeral casket even after the ceremony.

Some dogs are trained to help with medical needs and can detect a seizure or a trigger from PTSD, before the human. Additionally, they're taught what to do in the event of these emergencies to assist their humans until more help can be found.

I've met many cats designated as therapy animals, as they bring inner peace and love to those with mental illnesses. If patients rent, they can obtain a note from their doctor to permit them to have a pet, even if there is a no-pet policy.

Additionally, our pets can alert us to impending danger, often related to the weather, and we can console them during thunderstorms or fireworks.

It's obvious why people think, "I prefer my dog or cat to people. They listen, don't talk back, and provide unconditional love."

A friend of mine told me about how her mom has an uncanny connection with animals, which she developed while living on a farm. She has a large bay window facing her backyard, and birds would often fly into it. The smaller ones wouldn't survive, but one day, a much larger pileated Woodpecker crashed into it.

She could tell it was traumatized, so she brought it inside her home to let it get its bearings. When it was ready to leave, she let him fly away into the woods.

A day later, she kept hearing a pecking noise on her window that wouldn't stop. The woodpecker had returned. She felt it tried to thank her for the care! It wouldn't leave until she said, "You're welcome." It brought her immense joy, and they formed an unbelievable bond.

In this book, you'll focus on how to heal both you and/or your pet's trauma.

First, we'll go over what trauma really is, along with the different types of trauma and trauma responses. This clarity will help you uncover what's really going on and spot patterns when they show up in different situations.

In Chapter 2, it's time to discover more about empaths and how to get/stay in a more positive state, which will make everything in your life easier. There's also a special quiz to test if you're an empath yourself.

Because it can be hard to do things alone, next we'll talk about recruiting a 24/7 energetic A-Team composed of Archangels and guardian angels to help you heal and thrive.

Since life is all about energy, you'll learn to figure out exactly what you need to be in the best condition of your life (physically, mentally, emotionally, and spiritually). The team previously recruited will help you with this too.

From there, you'll discover additional tools to heal and thrive. We'll cover moon-based goal setting, manifesting, how to use a pendulum, essential oils, crystals, and most importantly, how to protect your energy.

Just like moths gravitate towards the light, you might get some energetic hang-ons trying to get their fill of your vibrant energy. I'll show you how to protect yourself from those (and who to call as your personal bouncer if they insist).

It helps to have a plan as it allows you to make clear decisions and avoid wasting time. What people don't know is that they were born with an instruction manual. In Chapter 6, we cover what makes you tick and which direction you planned for yourself before you were even born. We also cover how to spot inherited family issues so you can shake them and live your own life.

Then, to check how far you've come, Chapter 7 contains a quiz to see how much you've healed so far.

Are you ready to heal your trauma?

Once I healed my trauma, my life transformed. While my trauma is still part of my identity, it's now a source of pride and inner strength.

Looking back, I would ask myself, "How in the world did I get through that time in my life?" And it always amazed me and gave me a sense of accomplishment. Despite all of that, I turned out to be a responsible citizen and not a sociopath lacking empathy.

Overcoming trauma has increased my confidence and appreciation for life, and skyrocketed my personal growth.

It gave me the desire to help others who experienced the same traumatic events, and taught me to put my needs first so I'm actually capable of helping others.

My trauma allowed me to help people in many different ways.

Growing up, I was known as 'the voice of reason' whenever anyone needed advice. As a sounding board, I'd help my family or friends make difficult decisions, weigh pros and cons, decide their next steps, or validate their feelings related to a situation. Most importantly, I'd make them laugh when they felt down.

These qualities are why my career as a social worker came easily to me. I truly connected with my clients and started at their level of understanding.

With experience from my own upbringing, I helped mothers learn alternative ways of disciplining their children instead of physical abuse, and I could relate to the children's needs as victims. Those children were ultimately my clients.

I was able to help homeless mothers, as I was almost homeless during my divorce in California. We shared similar backgrounds, trying to make it on our own despite a lack of family support and money. The only thing that set me apart from my clients was my ability to obtain credit.

When I disclosed that I was a domestic violence survivor to my clients, it made them realize that it has nothing to do with them, their worth, or their status. It was never their fault that they were abused.

Sympathy overflowed for the underdog, because I think of how I'd feel if it were me. I'd take the new person under my wing and teach them the ropes, stuff that can't be learned in a textbook.

My principle is to be kind to those in need, because we never know their background or misfortunes. While guiding them, I taught many underprivileged women that they don't need money to have class. I'd teach them everything I didn't learn in life to help them get ahead, such as how to dress to impress, how to handle themselves in an interview, and how to manage time, money, and friendships.

If I didn't experience all those things in my life, I would never have been able to help as many people as I did. These experiences taught me that life is 100% about how we react to these traumatic events, not about the event itself.

With this book, I hope that you know you're not alone. That you'll be able to work through your trauma and turn this weakness into a source of strength. I hope that you learn more about yourself (self-knowledge is power) and understand not only why you acted the way you did, but that it's perfectly normal.

Let this book become your guide to move forward in your healing journey and to deepen your relationship with yourself, your higher self, others, and your community.

Wherever you may be, and whatever you may be going through, find new opportunities to shine your light. Speak your truth without being afraid of what anyone thinks of you (especially those online keyboard warriors hiding behind the anonymity of the internet).

I hope that you will gain confidence and become proud of your accomplishments, and help others experiencing similar situations.

Even in your darkest moments, remember that God truly loves you, as do his angels and your ancestors who are all helping you from heaven. They see you as a unique, precious, and beautiful soul.

Release your past to move toward the fantastic future awaiting you.

Once you work through your trauma, look forward to how self-love will change your life. If you can love yourself, then that love will attract loving opportunities for your career and relationships. Ultimately, you'll find true happiness.

Let's get started.

CHAPTER 1

WHAT IS TRAUMA?

Trauma is something I wouldn't wish on anyone, not even my worst enemy. It's the invisible virus that many of us endured and never fully recovered from, much less discussed.

Any emotionally troubling or life-threatening event creates trauma. It may consist of a series of incidents that adversely affect an individual's mental, physical, social, emotional, or spiritual well-being.[1] Furthermore, it can take over your life if unrecognized and unaddressed.

The National Library of Medicine stated that trauma easily gets misdiagnosed as ADHD, Depression, Anxiety, or Borderline Personality Disorder. This error happens because of the overlap of symptoms, or the psychologist focusing on the most obvious symptoms without digging deeper to discover why the patient's behavior occurs.

A fact less well-known related to trauma is that physical pain is linked to emotionally traumatic events.

It has become an epidemic, and these emotions remain trapped in your body for decades. You stay in fight-or-flight mode, unaware of the damage it causes you physically and emotionally. Trauma lingers underneath the surface. It creeps up on us, revealing itself through our physical health, emotions, actions, thoughts, self-image, and behaviors.

Trauma doesn't discriminate based on age, gender, socioeconomic status, race, ethnicity, or sexual orientation.

People struggle to heal from trauma, because they don't give themselves time to process the traumatic event and sweep it under the rug not realizing how it affects them long term. They numb their emotions through alcohol or drugs instead of dealing with them directly and working on their triggers.

According to The National Council for Mental Well-being, 223.4 million people, or 70% of adults, in the U.S. have experienced some trauma at least once in their lifetime.[2] As for abused or neglected children in the U.S., child welfare authorities report investigating the safety of more than 7.5 million kids annually.[3]

To break the cycle of abuse within families and end generational trauma, individuals and government organizations need to work together.

THE THREE TYPES OF TRAUMAS

It could be a one-time event that left a mark, or a long-term situation. The three types of trauma are acute, chronic, and complex trauma. Let's go over each one briefly.

Trauma Type # 1 - Acute Trauma

The first type is acute trauma, which refers to a one-time event such as an accident, being a victim of a crime, experiencing a natural disaster, the death of a loved one (including your pets or animals of any kind), facing a medical emergency, or undergoing a miscarriage.

Trauma Type # 2 - Chronic Trauma

The second type is chronic trauma, which encompasses any form of ongoing abuse, including child abuse and domestic violence. Chronic trauma usually comes from the actions of a specific person in a relationship.

Trauma Type # 3 - Complex Trauma

The third type is complex trauma, which is also long-term, characterized by ongoing issues that involve more than one type of abuse. Complex trauma happens through various events that seem to occur one after another, such as medical emergencies, homelessness, mental health problems, or substance abuse.

Regardless of which type of trauma you suffer from, it can lead to feeling anxious, angry, afraid, depressed, and guilty. These emotions fuel addiction, cause mental health diagnoses, create challenges in relationships, and can even become the source of chronic illnesses or cancer.

Emotionally, the trauma victim might feel numb and unable to experience love or joy. Irritation and anger take over as they struggle to cope with their wide range of emotions. Some struggle to control their loud outbursts or may instigate unnecessary fights.

Overall, these victims suffer from low self-esteem, a lack of intimacy, and many have lost their ability to trust completely.

TRAUMA RESPONSES

What's a traumatic response? It's an automatic, often involuntary reaction to a physically or emotionally harmful event. Your body protects itself from perceived danger.

Because your mind specializes in spotting patterns to keep you safe, when traumatized, this goes into overdrive. Anything even remotely resembling your trauma causes an instant (and often excessive) reaction.

Think about how cats shoot away from cucumbers the minute they spot them. They aren't afraid of the cucumbers, but even the slightest resemblance to a snake triggers an autoresponse. In this case, the reaction doesn't stem from an individual cat's experience, but a survival mechanism inherited by an entire species. The cats who experienced the danger and survived passed their warning system down to their descendants.

The problem starts when this protection overprotects you from something that wasn't threatening you to begin with.

Several trauma responses exist. The four most common ones are fight, flight, freeze, and fawn. While each one incites very different reactions, all four impact your thinking, behaviors, and ability to be independent. I call it being in 'survivor mode'.

The Fight Response

The fight trauma response is automatic and triggered by a perceived threat, causing the body to activate the nervous system. This causes a surge of energy often expressed through anger, aggression, or the need to protect oneself.

People feel threatened and start yelling, throwing things, kicking whatever they can, and acting irrationally to protect themselves. Usually, it's an overreaction to something minor. Animals will display their reactions to threats by hissing, growling, barking, charging, or biting.

A friend of mine from grade school got caught toilet papering someone's yard. The male owner came out, grabbed her, and tried to bring her inside his house. My friend screamed 'rape' very loudly to get someone's attention or help from the neighbors. She was trapped inside this man's home when the police arrived. This friend had a history of abuse.

While she didn't consciously initiate a fight response, she recognized her boundaries were crossed and tried to save herself from further abuse.

A good example of an animal displaying a fight trauma response is when my little, fifteen-pound dog charges a big deer in our yard. His fear triggers his adrenaline, and he automatically tries to defend himself by barking and charging at the deer. Luckily for him, they do run away.

The Flight Response

Similar to the fight trauma responses, the flight response is automatic, and adrenaline spikes. However, here they'll try to leave the situation that they consider a threat to them physically or emotionally.

People make a split-second decision to flee from even the smallest resemblance to their perceived danger. This reaction could be as simple as someone running from their abuser or an animal fleeing from a larger animal that could cause them harm.

For example, an abused child may hear a kitchen drawer opening and the sound of a spatula. This child knows they'll be reprimanded and hit with this spatula, so they run and hide under the bed.

Animals will do the same. When a cat can hear other cats fighting and screeching, they run the other way to keep themselves safe.

The Freeze Response

The freeze trauma response happens when fighting or fleeing isn't an option in front of the perceived danger. Perhaps a child knows they can't fight back or run fast enough, so their body goes into full panic mode, numbing them from moving out of danger.

An example of a typical freeze trauma response for humans would be during physical or sexual abuse. The victim goes numb, freezes their emotions, and disassociates their thoughts as a protective mechanism during the actual traumatic event.

You can witness this response when observing the behaviors of bunnies or squirrels. They hear a noise, perceive danger, and stay completely still as if they're a statue or even pretend to be dead until the threat is gone.

The Fawn Response

The fawn trauma response is when an individual decides to become a 'people pleaser' to avoid conflict and minimize the chance of attack.

Humans use this response in a domestic violence situation to avoid ruffling the abuser's feathers and maintain peace to protect themselves from harm. My coping mechanism was to please my mom as a child. I wanted to be helpful so I wouldn't get in trouble. When she called me "mommy's little helper," I knew I was safe for a little while.

An animal using this response becomes submissive to defer potential danger from another aggressive animal. They will lower their posture, avoid eye contact, or put their tail between their legs. This behavior tells the other animal that they have no intention of fighting.

Dogs at a dog park learn quickly how to behave to avoid encouraging a physical attack from another dog. They know that if they become submissive, back away, and walk the other way, they will remain safe.

Trauma Responses

Different Ways They Can Reveal Themselves

Fight
- Increased Irritability
- Anger Outbursts
- Assertively Critical of Others
- Seeks Power and Control
- Impulsive Decision Making
- Inability to Hear Other POV's

Flight
- Hyperactive or Avoidant
- Always 'Busy' or 'On the Go'
- Constant Overthinking
- Increased Anxiety or Panic
- Perfectionistic Tendencies
- Overworking or Workaholic

Freeze
- Feeling Overwhelmed
- Lack of Boundaries
- Often Codependent
- Low Self-Esteem
- Lack of Identity
- People-Pleasing Behavior
- Easily Exploited by Others

Fawn
- Feeling Detached or Lifeless
- Feeling Physically Stuck
- Difficulty Making Decisions
- Dissociation or Spacing Out
- Self-Isolation or Avoidance
- Depression or Feeling Low
- Feelings of Shame

MPH

Some other responses include losing hope for the future. Without hope, there's no desire to live. The traumatized can become detached, even losing a sense of concern for others, because they're in survival mode.

They may struggle to concentrate or make decisions and frequently feel jumpy, becoming startled quickly by sudden noises that could be related to their triggers.

Less-obvious trauma symptoms are easily overlooked, such as feelings of guilt or shame, paranoia, and not maintaining long-term relationships. Trauma is a violation of personal safety and comfort. Therefore, the victim may be reluctant to trust again or allow themselves to be disrespected, because they feel they aren't worthy of having their boundaries respected.

Many don't realize that a loss of self is a trauma symptom, especially if it happens during childhood. This disconnect occurs when basic survival skills take precedence over normal self-development.

Have you ever known someone who constantly apologizes for no reason? That default reaction is a trauma response.

Have you found yourself over-explaining to ensure your side of the story was heard? This anxiety is a trauma response rooted in being ignored or misunderstood as a child.

I've found myself feeling guilty when I relax, which is another trauma response. As a child, if I relaxed, I'd have to do extra chores because I wasn't busy enough.

The most obvious sign of a trauma victim is being a people pleaser, like me. One of the biggest fears is that people will hate you (or worse, leave you). To get them to like and stay with us, we avoid saying no or even change our way of being/ dressing to not displease them. We also want to prevent others from experiencing the same difficulties we did.

This behavior stems from the fact that the love from our abuser wasn't unconditional. We needed to earn it and could lose it at any time, so we felt lucky to receive even scraps of attention.

At 19 years old, just before Christmas, my mom told my dad I had to move out of the family home within two weeks. I worked as a waitress and went to college full-time. My mom didn't like that I was never home.

She herself was kicked out of her home at 16.

It was Christmas break, and I ended up moving on New Year's Eve on a snowy night. My dad was the only one who helped me move my stuff after he got home from work.

Once I moved out, I would either visit too much or not enough. Either way, I could never win.

Then, my mom decided to move from Cincinnati to California and begged me to come. I didn't really want to, but she insisted until I agreed. She even promised to pay for me to move back if I didn't like it.

While I was unaware at the time, her arguments were full of lies and half-truths (I hated living there, and she took her words back).

My mother scheduled the move the day after my 21st birthday. She had my car, money, and clothing. Since she was in charge, and I wasn't ready at 6 a.m. as planned, my dad called to say they were leaving with my mom screaming in the background. I felt helpless and humiliated, believing I was so unlovable that they could abandon me like an old piece of furniture they no longer wanted.

As an empath, I got used to sensing her deep jealousy and hatred toward me, and each time, I'd emotionally shut down.

It wasn't until about six hours later that they called back to say I needed to meet them in Kansas City, MO. To get there, I had to take a Greyhound Bus that changed buses in the middle of the night, and I'd arrive the following day at 8 a.m. I had to trust they'd be there to pick me up, as I didn't have any money and was completely vulnerable.

Waiting felt like pure torture. I sat there contemplating how I would survive on my own: would I become a prostitute or addicted to drugs? Would I be homeless? I was beside myself, but I kept all my anger close to my heart since there was no one to talk to, and I wouldn't anyway, out of pure shame (which is one of the lowest frequencies on the vibrational chart referenced in chapter 2).

After a three-hour wait, my mother allowed my dad to pick me up. It was 11 a.m.! He said she didn't want to be woken up early or inconvenienced because of me.

Imagine my humiliation when I returned to visit my hometown, and everyone knew about my parents abandoning me! Not just close friends, but even acquaintances said they were sorry to hear about my parents moving without me. Quickly, I hid my embarrassment by laughing it off and said, "You can't pick your family, only your friends."

Nobody taught me this method. It was my way of coping with the fact that my parents didn't love me. This situation wasn't the only time I felt abandoned, traumatized, ashamed, or unsafe, but I pushed it under the rug to deal with it many, many years later.

In a perfect world, my father would have saved me. However, he was co-dependent on my mother, who called all the shots. He wasn't going to be my hero because my mom treated him the same as me. This man couldn't save himself from the web of dysfunction, let alone help his four children.

TRADITIONAL TRAUMA TREATMENTS

There are traditional ways to treat trauma, such as psychotherapy, cognitive behavioral therapy, hypnotherapy, and medications.

A new treatment designed explicitly for PTSD is called EMDR, Eye Movement Desensitization and Reprocessing, and I've witnessed massive results firsthand.

Especially helpful for anxiety, there's a therapy called EFT tapping. Emotional Freedom Techniques are great to do every night before bed, as the tapping targets the meridian points, similar to acupuncture or acupressure. It helps release tension, allowing you to sink into a more comfortable state.

Additionally, there are simple techniques to help you regulate your nervous system, linked to the Vagus nerve that runs throughout your body, from your head to your feet.

Another traditional way to heal from trauma includes releasing endorphins through exercise or practicing yoga.

About thirty years ago, when my friend began teaching yoga, she noticed that her new students often left her class in tears halfway through. It wasn't until a few years later that a neuroscientist discovered yoga releases stored and trapped emotions, leading the body to release them through tears automatically. It's a profoundly enlightening experience, and soon, yoga became the preferred exercise for those on a spiritual healing journey.

SECONDHAND TRAUMA

It took me over twenty years of working with traumatized clients as a social worker to understand the adverse effects of trauma on a person's body, both physically and emotionally. During that time, I frequently experienced secondhand trauma as I listened to my clients' horrific stories about how they arrived at their current circumstances.

Secondhand trauma can result from watching the news, witnessing a horrific crime, or even seeing a violent movie. Throughout my career,

I've heard thousands of stories, and it took a toll on my mental health and stress levels.

Throughout the last three years of my career, I learned about Trauma-Informed Care while working with clients who had lost custody of their children.

The goal was to help parents feel safe while building trust, which can be challenging to establish, as they may have been disappointed in the past by broken promises from previous professionals. Another essential way to empower them is by offering choices regarding how they'd like to heal, and I'd work to make that happen.

The ultimate objective was to avoid re-traumatizing the client while helping them achieve their goals.

By no means do I want to compare a traumatized human to a traumatized pet, but veterinarians are now undertaking Fear-Free training to find ways to help pets feel safe enough for services, similar to Trauma-Informed Care for humans.

My first three years of social work were at Children's Services in the Ongoing department, which meant that I was monitoring the parents for possible abuse. This assignment is where I first heard of secondhand trauma, but I wasn't aware of its effects on my body.

Due to high caseloads, I neglected myself by eating unhealthy foods and failing to visit the doctor or dentist for preventive care. I also stopped exercising while working long hours. I aged tremendously during that time. Add 17 more years to the equation, plus my childhood trauma, and I felt like I survived a war, which ultimately forced me to retire to come up for air. I left that job for the sake of my sanity.

I took the traditional route to heal my trauma until I hit a dead end with counselors and medication, but there were no other options at that time.

It felt like I had to do everything in life on my own because there were consequences if I asked for help. These consequences are why trauma victims are hyper-independent. They needed to do everything without an adult's guidance.

My trauma continued as I married young while living in California to escape my abusive parents. Unbeknownst to me, my new husband was similar to my mother, a common occurrence.

When dating, it's not that you look for this type of person. These people seek you out for your kindness and high vibration, knowing they can control you. Of course, you don't see the red flags until they manipulate you into a relationship, and it gets worse from there. However, it's possible to heal, which allows you to recognize these red flags in advance.

After divorcing and healing, I discovered that my ex-husband was an overt narcissist.

This type of narcissist is characterized by an exaggerated ego and a preoccupation with status, wealth, flattery, and power due to their grandiosity and sense of entitlement. In contrast, the covert narcissist, like my mother, tends to be introverted and passive-aggressive, although capable of being just as manipulative and also lacking empathy and compassion. They often wear several masks to conceal their insecurities.

I was afraid to remarry because I didn't trust myself enough to make the right decision.

Thankfully, after a lot of healing, I found someone who is the polar opposite of a narcissist. I told myself I wouldn't settle and wanted a partner who was equally involved and committed to the relationship.

SUFFERING IN SILENCE

Those painful experiences happened fifty years ago, and I wish I had learned what I know now at a much younger age. Nobody talked about mental health back then.

Another reason I wrote this book is to raise awareness in society about couples who are childless not by choice, which causes ongoing trauma throughout their entire lifetime.

"Approximately 1 in 6 people have experienced infertility at some point in their lives, according to the World Health Organization, and an estimated 17.5% of people worldwide have experienced infertility." Research shows it's one of the primary reasons for divorce, as it can negatively impact couples' psychological, financial, physical, and emotional health.

Some people who wish to start a family but are unable to conceive find that infertility complications affect their mental health and overall quality of life.

As you can see, many people are suffering in silence. Why? Because society hasn't normalized talking about it yet, and the general public doesn't know how to respond, especially when miscarriages or deaths are involved.

In my experience, unaware couples who talk about their children constantly don't understand the grief it causes infertile couples. Asking whether you have children is a simple question, but it's hard for me to answer. Do I say yes, but they're in heaven? Do I say anything at all?

Alternatively, asking when you plan to have children is also considered a rude question and feels like complete torture. I learned to say, "Unfortunately, I don't have children." Then, as we get older, the next question is, "Do you have grandchildren?" There are many triggers for infertile couples that affect their ability to cope, especially each and every holiday.

I've known women who were admitted to the psychiatric unit due to suicidal thoughts related to miscarrying a child.

I understand this intense feeling. The loss is significant after trying for so long. Each month, imagine hoping for a miracle and then being disappointed again, month after month. I experienced seven years of infertility, three miscarriages, including twins, two husbands, and many years in between.

Wellbutrin saved my life because, when my journey was over and the realization sank in that I'd never be a mother, I was suicidal. I didn't want to live anymore without experiencing motherhood. What's the use of living when you can't live through the innocent eyes of your offspring?

It wasn't until we got a puppy, and then another puppy two years later, that I truly began to heal. They made sure I felt like a mom with our daily routine. I brushed them every morning, fed them, and consoled them during fireworks or thunderstorms. Many people say to get a puppy before having kids, because they make for great practice and, unlike kids, they never grow up.

After healing, I regained my motivation, and I've learned to live without being a mother. It's possible, but only with the support of other couples facing similar challenges who understand you, and loving creatures who fill that void in your heart.

Due to the general lack of awareness, I joined an organization called Childless Not By Choice and submitted articles to promote a better understanding of the subject. I also started a Meetup group for men and women who are childless not by choice, and we support one another, especially during the holidays.

My goal has been accomplished if I can help even one person heal from their trauma.

Knowledge is power, and learning is a natural progression through life. I found that I leaned on my spirituality even as a young child, although I didn't understand my experiences until I was older. I developed a relationship with my guardian angels, and they were the answer to my prayers. I will discuss this topic in detail in Chapter Three.

While there are many holistic ways to treat trauma, use these tools in conjunction with traditional help.

Trauma can also have other consequences, like developing or strengthening skills to survive. People become empaths as a result of trauma; therefore, the empath easily understands others' feelings and pinpoints their cause. Like changes in the weather, they are hypersensitive to changes in the atmosphere of a room or house.

A downside is that empaths feel emotions more strongly and can absorb the emotions of their abuser as the trauma is occurring. I could feel my mother's hatred for me through her words and actions. A harsh voice yelling at an empath can feel like an emotional lashing.

Do you think you might be an empath? In the next chapter, we'll go into more detail, and you can take a quiz to find out.

CHAPTER 2

WHY EMPATHS, LIGHTWORKERS & OTHER HEALING PROFESSIONALS?

Did you know that being an empath is a natural response to trauma? An empath is someone who feels other people's emotions and can put themselves in others' shoes to the point of it becoming unhealthy. This blurring of boundaries occurs because the empath not only feels the emotions but also absorbs those feelings as if they were their own. This energy absorption is not intentional; it depends on the empath's sensitivity.

Being an empath is a learned skill often developed in childhood to protect oneself, or even as an adult while living as a domestic violence victim.

As a child, I had to determine if it was safe to leave my bedroom many times. To do so, I used all six senses to gauge the energy temperature in the room, and I still do this today.

In the physical plane, I listened for any signs of distress, always looked before I leaped, and sniffed to gather more clues, such as whether someone was smoking or cooking. I even tasted the leftover liquid in an abandoned cup to see if there was alcohol involved.

Additionally, within my body, I sensed a gut instinct, akin to a sixth sense, whenever danger was near.

This gut reaction evolved into intuition, a skill that develops over time, enabling you to know things before they happen. By the time I reached my teenage years, I had become quite skilled at being a detective in my own home.

As an adult empath, I could tell what people were thinking based on their facial expressions, body language, tone of voice, or actions. I could sense their pain without them having to say a word, and I often imagined what it would be like to walk in their shoes. This skill is why I had so much success as a social worker; I was always one step ahead of my clients.

Later in life, unknowingly, I absorbed other people's physical symptoms as well.

During a visit to my cousin's house, who has lupus, I asked her why I felt nauseated, as if I was going to lose my cookies. She mentioned that she usually experiences that feeling, but she felt great. Her acknowledgement confirmed my suspicion that I absorbed her physical pain, but at the time, I thought it happened because we were close.

It became a significant issue when I worked at the Council on Aging with elderly clients who suffered from extreme pain. I would go home with the same problems, without realizing what was happening.

A friend of mine had carpal tunnel surgery on her wrist, and that same day, I had to wrap my wrist in gauze to prevent it from moving, as it caused pain.

Absorbing others' pain didn't seem like a big deal until I was doing a home visit with a client to supervise her visitation with her child, who was in the custody of JFS.

Because she was only allowed two hours a week to see her child, she didn't want to go to the hospital despite experiencing extreme vaginal bleeding. I instantly knew she was having a miscarriage, even though she wasn't aware she was pregnant. She refused to go to the hospital, and soon, I had to leave for my next meeting.

When I returned to the office, I felt very shaky, nauseated, and weak to the point that I had to go home.

Once at home, I realized that despite not having a menstrual period for three years, I had vaginal bleeding. It felt as if I had experienced a miscarriage, too.

I was beside myself, and when I explained this to a friend, she said that I might have saved my client's life due to her extreme blood loss. My body automatically took it on without me even realizing it. That was my last job as a social worker, as I couldn't continue in my career, nor did I want to.

It became my mission to protect my energy.

I purchased a David Vogel crystal with two half-triangles stacked on top of each other, forming a barrier against the energy of others. Worn with the flat side facing outward, it dispels energy. If I flip it around, the energy gets amplified.

It's beneficial to amplify the energy when receiving energy healings or connecting with angels, although its primary purpose is to keep me mentally and physically safe. Since that day, I wear this necklace every time I visit my cousin for the weekend.

There are more ways to protect your energy, which we'll discuss in the following chapters.

Before that, below is a quiz, along with scoring instructions, to help determine if you're an empath. This quiz will provide you with a deeper understanding of what it means to be an empath.

EMPATH QUIZ

1. Are you considered a good listener?
2. Do you have trouble saying no because you feel guilty?
3. Do you feel a home should be your sanctuary?
4. Have people accused you of being "overly sensitive" or too emotional?
5. Do you frequently get overwhelmed or anxious?
6. Are people you don't even know sharing very personal stories with you?
7. Do arguments or yelling make you feel ill and/or leave you shaking?
8. Do you absorb the stress and moods of those around you?
9. Do crowds drain you, and do you need alone time to recharge?
10. When socializing, do you prefer 1-on-1 interactions and small groups over big parties?
11. Does it stress you out when the music is so loud you can't have a proper conversation?
12. Do you enjoy being alone in nature because you finally don't have to worry about what anyone else is feeling or thinking?
13. Do you overanalyze your words to minimize conflict?
14. Do you tend to give too much in relationships?
15. Are you worried about losing yourself in intimate relationships?
16. Do you love animals and bond with them quickly? (Does it feel like they understand you better than humans can?)
17. Do you tend to be too nice and end up getting taken advantage of?

18. Do you need a long time to recuperate after dealing with difficult people/ energy vampires?
19. Do you feel others' physical pain as if it were yours?
20. Do you feel like you don't fit in and are different from others?

NOW CALCULATE YOUR RESULTS:

If you answered yes to one to five questions, you're at least partially an empath.

Responding 'yes' to six to 10 questions indicates moderate empathic tendencies.

Responding 'yes' to 11 to 15 indicates strong empathic tendencies.

Answering yes to more than 15 questions means that you are a full-blown empath.

If you identify as an empath, you're likely a lightworker who serves others and the planet as your life's purpose.

People from all walks of life, including doctors, nurses, life coaches, and many other healing professions, can be lightworkers. They spread positivity, love, and healing energy in the world, and their primary task is to transmute darkness into light.

To achieve this, they experienced difficult circumstances and found ways to overcome their darkness.

Now they use those experiences to help others rise above their trauma.

Because of their spiritual connection to a higher power and radiant aura, they attract many individuals with lower energies, such as narcissists. These individuals seek the energy of empaths or lightworkers without wanting to evolve. They are known as energy vampires because they only thrive around empaths, absorbing their kindness and leaving the empath feeling depleted.

I identify as a lightworker because I firmly believe that transforming darkness into light is my life purpose, and I should help my fellow lightworkers, which is another reason why I wrote this book.

If you identify as an empath, you likely love pets, as pets are empaths as well.

Animals attune to our energy, and we can feel their love! They teach us how to love unconditionally and live in the present, often without us realizing it. Additionally, they teach us by mirroring our behavior. For example, if they sense your anxiety, they may become anxious themselves. They may reflect physical behavior, like adopting the same limp, or absorb your pain.

If you're supposed to rest, your pet will run around energetically and later regret it due to discomfort. This action is how animals say, 'Listen to the doctor's orders'.

Sometimes, they will act contrary to what you want them to do, such as greeting a stranger. They might bark and lunge if they sense your discomfort with the interaction, or they may hide behind your leg, imitating shy behavior to show how absurd it appears. They will go to great lengths to teach us, and they always give back 110% love and loyalty.

All other healing professionals may be empaths or absorb their clients' emotions (often without realizing it), as their professions typically require empathy. These professions include doctors, nurses, veterinarians, social workers, counselors, and even hair stylists.

During COVID-19, many doctors who worked in the hospitals committed suicide due to feelings of helplessness and being overwhelmed by witnessing so many dying patients. Veterinarians are at risk, too. According to the National Library of Medicine, the suicide rate in the veterinary profession has been estimated to be close to twice that of the dental profession, more than twice that of the medical profession, and four times higher than the general population.[4]

Veterans face an alarmingly high suicide rate because of the traumas they've experienced. Many are diagnosed with Post-Traumatic Stress Disorder. Statistics show that approximately 18 veterans take their own lives each day in the United States.[5]

"One study of more than 1000 random psychologists found that 62% of them self-identified as depressed. Of those with depressive symptoms, 42% reported experiencing some form of suicidal ideation or behavior."[6] Registered nurses are 64% more likely to commit suicide compared to non-healthcare workers.[7] Also, "The results of a logistic analysis found that being a social worker increased the odds of death by suicide by 55.6%, compared to the rest of the working-age population."[8]

As a social worker, I worked at a 24-hour suicide hotline, and I was stunned by how many people I worked with suffered from suicidal thoughts. Science confirmed my suspicions: the people trying to save others were drowning in their own emotions.[9]

The agency found that the number of calls increased when the weather changed in the fall. Perhaps this was due to the anticipation of cold weather approaching or the impending holidays, but it's a time you wouldn't expect a suicide. Additionally, call frequency increased during full moons, as people experienced mood changes from the moon's gravitational pull.[10]

Throughout my career as a social worker, I always knew when there was a full moon because many of my clients would sabotage their progress, forcing them to start all over again.

Humans absorb negative emotions. Therefore, it's essential to work on their emotional vibrational frequency.

Each emotion vibrates at a specific frequency level: the higher the frequency, the better it is for physical, mental, and spiritual health. In numerical terms, the chart below illustrates how high a person's vibration can be in response to their positive emotions.

The lowest level is 20, experienced by those who feel shame, while the highest is 700, associated with feeling enlightened. The goal is to raise the body's vibration to alleviate negative emotions, which are trapped energy that can lead to disease.

Raising your vibration requires clearing and dissolving negative emotions, which may require a complete lifestyle change. Self-love is key. Below are some suggestions.

30 WAYS TO RAISE YOUR VIBRATION

1. Show Gratitude
2. Hydrate with water
3. Journal away cares
4. Declutter and organize
5. Perform acts of kindness
6. Cuddle
7. Spend time with pets/ animals
8. Reach out instead of isolating
9. Take an Epsom Salt/ Bubble Bath
10. Pause when needed
11. Learn something new
12. Spend time by/in/on water
13. Breathe Deeply
14. Chat with a friend
15. Spend time in nature
16. Dance, skip, hike
17. Listen to music
18. Meditate
19. Pray
20. Balance your chakras
21. Walk barefoot (on the beach)
22. Nurture yourself
23. Hug a tree
24. Sing
25. Get a good night's sleep
26. Laugh a lot, smile, or joke
27. Release perfection
28. Exercise or do yoga
29. Serve a greater good
30. Wear crystal jewelry

Fortunately, we can control our thoughts and consciously choose to vibrate at a higher level. Each thought connects to an emotion that affects our behavior and dictates whether we lead a peaceful or low-frequency life.

The first step to being more aware of your vibration is to ensure you're grounded. To be grounded, one must be emotionally stable, calm, connected to reality, and down-to-earth. Essentially, it's when you quiet your mind and your thoughts are in the present moment.

When my teacher taught me how to ground myself, she told me to stand tall and imagine the soles of my feet had roots growing into the ground.

Although it didn't initially make sense to me, you know you're grounded if you can feel all your energy drop down to your feet, which happens when you walk barefoot on grass.

I remember as a child thinking it was electrifying because grounding with the earth offers a sensory experience that stimulates the nerve endings on the bottom of your feet. This stimulation releases endorphins that promote well-being, decrease anxiety, and provide a sense of connection to the earth.

Did you know that forest spirituality refers to the deep connection and spiritual significance individuals experience when interacting with forests? This experience includes feeling a sense of awe, a connection to nature, and a deeper understanding of the world.

Forests reconnect us with our roots, enhancing the effectiveness of our senses. Everything is more intense when we walk along the forest trail in the shade of the trees. The colors are more vivid, the smells stronger, the grass softer, and the birdsong is more enticing.

Immersing yourself leads to feelings of peacefulness, which is considered a form of being grounded, and increases your vibrational rate.

Luckily, when I was a child, my family would go camping every weekend and on a two-week road trip every year. We'd drive to different places in the U.S. This was a godsend. Nature saved me emotionally, and I didn't even know it. Perhaps that's how I survived my abusive childhood, as it kept me grounded.

The concept of being grounded is so popular that grounding mats are now sold for indoor use, allowing you to sit at your desk with your feet on the mat. Many people reported sleeping better, with decreased stress and pain, and elevated moods.

We're just getting started on how to learn to heal from trauma through spiritual tools. Next, we learn to rely on our angels for guidance, which helps keep us safe and calm, thereby experiencing less stress through faith.

CHAPTER 3

Angelic Assistance

There are times in life when you feel utterly alone. You hide the pain in your heart, paste on a smile, and cling to the ticking of the clock like a lifeline — just to make it through the day. It feels like no one is capable of or willing to understand how you feel.

But did you know?

No matter how low you feel, no matter the place or the hour, there's someone who will always reach out and help. Always ready and able to be in many places at once, they want to know how they can help you or your pet.

Let me show you who to call, how to call them, and how to listen for their answer.

Archangel Raphael - The Divine Healer

Did you know there is an Archangel who can assist you with healing your body, mind, and soul?

Yes, it's the omnipresent Archangel Raphael, shining emerald green light on your aura in times of need. Invoking calmness and peace, call on him especially during moments of intense stress or panic. His name means 'God will heal,' and he's one of the top four archangels who serve as messengers of God.

Archangel Raphael is renowned for his extraordinary healing powers and is often associated with clairvoyance. He can help find animals if they are lost or in need of healing.

Many remain unaware that he can help awaken the third eye, enabling them to perceive angels, their signs, and the divine energy surrounding them.

He supports lightworkers who require his healing to release the fear, trauma, and guilt that hinder their intuitive visions.

Feelings of shame can emerge if someone judges your spiritual beliefs. You fear seeing something frightening or uncovering a repressed memory from your past. The more you collaborate with archangels, the more you will trust them.

It's essential to have spiritual guidance during challenging times and moments of healing. However, you must always ask for an angel's assistance. They can't help unless you specifically request it, as it would interfere with your free will.

The only angel you don't need to call is your guardian angel, whose job is to keep you physically safe, and they will automatically act on this if needed.

When asking for assistance, say whatever you feel in your heart. It can be more generic, like: "Please send me healing in all areas of my life." Or you can be specific and state you'd like assistance with healing your layers of trauma or even physical pain.

Whether you're physically ill, struggling emotionally or financially, or facing complicated relationships or addictions, Archangel Raphael is always available for you. He makes a great partner for empaths, lightworkers, or other healing professionals.

Don't worry about depriving others; he can be in many places at once. Simply ask for what you need.

While working with Archangel Raphael, you may find yourself drawn to the color green, as I was. I didn't make the connection at first because I always associated red with the heart. However, green represents the heart chakra.

Gradually, I bought a green coat, wallet, and a sweater, even though it's not my favorite color. That's when I realized my heart had begun to heal from my trauma. Soon, my heart chakra became wide open, which was my ultimate goal.

When I started working with Archangel Raphael as an animal healer, I'd call on him to help pets release stuck energy caused by trauma during my sessions. I hear his wings tapping on the walls or window sills whenever he is present.

Shortlist him if you're a healer because he never disappoints. With his assistance, I've noticed that my healing sessions are much stronger. Imagine what he can do for you!

Archangel Michael – The Heavenly Bodyguard

Archangel Michael is the leader of all angels and the most powerful. Both shield and sword, he protects whoever calls on him.

Emotionally, he provides you with integrity, courage, and the strength to face life's challenges. It takes courage to reach your goals, even when taking lots of baby steps. Let him support you with any fear-inducing task, such as public speaking, interviewing, meeting new friends, having hard conversations, etc.

On a physical level, he intervenes in miraculous ways to save lives.

Call on this travel angel whenever you step into a vehicle, train, or plane, as he will protect you the most. He can also protect your pet from harm, from accidents if lost, and even from negative energies inside your home.

Archangel Michael saved my life while I was a passenger in a vehicle driving on the San Francisco bridge during rush hour.

Even though the direction of the lanes changed with a sign featuring a huge X above, some drivers still didn't notice. A powerful voice told me to ' Get in the other lane'. I screamed it three times before the driver finally switched lanes, and we narrowly avoided a head-on collision.

Additionally, I always advise clients that if they're walking down the street and feel frightened by a group of people approaching, they should say, "Michael, I need you now!" You'll be surprised when the group turns and walks the other way.

Safety is his specialty, which is why many military personnel wear his pendant around their necks for protection.

You may feel a sense of security and comfort or see royal blue and purple light shine on you when he's near.

Archangel Gabriel – The Soul Communicator

Another powerful Archangel is Gabriel, known for delivering messages from God and serving as a beacon of hope, and offering solace to those with emotional or soul-based wounds.

Here's an example of how to invite Archangel Gabriel to heal your trauma: "Archangel Gabriel, I humbly invite your beautiful white light of peace to fill my body and bring healing to my wounds."

Archangel Gabriel and Mother Mary work together closely to minister to sensitive children. They guide in matters of conception, adoption, pregnancy, and birth. Because Gabriel is deeply concerned with children's welfare, he mentors responsible and loving adults who wish to assist the young.

He also helps women suffering from sexual trauma or psychic attacks when they call on him. As he's a being of love and light, he doesn't judge. He'll embrace you no matter what you went through.

Archangel Uriel – The "Tough Love" Life Coach

Archangel Uriel is the angel of wisdom and helps you make the best possible decision in any situation. He helps you transform yourself and your life and heal from emotional trauma.

If you're feeling stuck or creatively blocked, he guides you to heal every aspect of your life by transforming disappointments into victories and finding blessings in adversity.

This loyal supporter helps you deepen your faith, enabling you to release destructive thoughts, resentment, and bitterness.

Archangel Uriel guides people to make decisions aligned with divine wisdom and encourages them to see the light, even in difficulty. Call on him when you need to resolve conflicts or desire clarity during life-changing decisions.

Archangel Chamuel – The Love Doctor

Archangel Chamuel, known as the angel of love, is a kind-hearted and compassionate being who assists with matters of the heart and relationships. He helps expand your heart chakra and ignite a flame of love within you.

In need of a job aligned with your heart and soul? Call the Love Doctor to form a divine connection and find a career you'll love.

When you call upon him, he helps you find inner peace, resolve conflicts with others, mend existing relationships, forgive those who hurt you, and deepen romantic connections.

He's the invisible hug you didn't know you needed, helping you heal when you lose a pet or loved one.

Archangel Raziel – The Dream and Past Life Interpreter

Archangel Raziel helps with personal growth, interpreting dreams and past lives, and finding creative ideas and solutions. Use the nightly whispers of your soul and the cries from your past to choose a new path, with each step bringing you closer to the life of your dreams.

Call on this angel if you need help figuring out life's direction or meaning, and why certain challenges are unfolding in your life.

Archangel Haniel – The Joy Finder

Archangel Haniel is the Archangel of Intuition. She helps you fine-tune your inner guidance system so you can recognize, pursue, and obtain what brings you the most joy.

Archangel Zadkiel – The Peacemaker

Known as the Archangel of forgiveness, Zadkiel helps release anger and resentment, whether directed at others or yourself, to heal your relationships and support your spiritual evolution.

Archangel Jophiel – The Beauty Spotter

Archangel Jophiel is associated with creativity, overcoming negative thoughts, and seeing the beauty in the world. She helps interior decorators, artists, and anyone seeking to bring beauty and harmony into their environment.

GUARDIAN ANGELS

Guardian angels are celestial beings who have never incarnated on Earth. Assigned to you before conception, they come with knowledge of your life plan. While for most things, they need your permission to step in, they will intervene without you asking for help if it isn't your time to leave this earth.

I experienced this firsthand while white-water rafting with other college students.

The instructors seemed apprehensive, making me nervous, and we just went through a rough spot (I found out later it was one of the highest class waves).

Suddenly, I was thrown ten feet out of the boat into the water. Plunged into raging waters, I couldn't tell which way was up or down as I flailed around. Meanwhile, a vision flashed before my eyes of a newspaper spinning, and the headline read: *UC Student Dies in White-Water Rafting Accident.*

That snapped me out of it. I realized that I was underwater and might drown, and my blood ran cold. I didn't want to die.

While struggling for air, I felt someone grab the back of my life jacket, and my head popped above water.

As I looked around, there wasn't a human nearby, only me floating on my back with my feet forward through the high waves. Unable to fight the current, I could only wait for the next boat to rescue me. Luckily, my guardian angels stayed with me until I reached the shore.

It was all videotaped. I was shocked to see that the person flying in the air was me! Miraculously, despite not wearing a helmet, I suffered no injuries.

Pets – Fluffy Guardian Angels

Many people believe that pets are guardian angels without wings, serving as protectors. Their energy frequency is higher than that of humans, as they've mastered unconditional love.

Dogs are the only animals that love us more than they love themselves.

Pets vibrate at a frequency only one level lower than an angel, which is why I consider pets to be our Earth angels! They can choose to be an official guardian angel once they cross over the rainbow bridge, though I believe their spirit never truly leaves.

My cat, Princess, died at 21, but her face comes to me in visions, and at times, I can feel and hear her purring on my leg.

Angels And Chakras

Everything is energy, but your fears and experiences can block the flow. Your chakras are energy centers, each with a very specific function.

For now, see below a chart that outlines the seven chakras in the human body and identifies which angel helps you open which energy center to support your healing and energetic alignment. Each chakra corresponds to a color, which also represents the angel associated. In the next chapter, you'll examine the chakras in more detail.

Crown ~ White ~ Archangel Raziel

Third Eye ~ Indigo ~ Archangel Zadkiel

Throat ~ Blue ~ Archangel Haniel

Heart ~ Green ~ Archangel Chamuel

Solar Plexus ~ Yellow ~ Archangel Jophiel

Sacral ~ Orange ~ Archangel Gabriel

Root ~ Red ~ Archangel Michael

Calling All Angels – How To Ask For Help

You may be wondering how to contact your angels for assistance. It can be formal or informal, as long as you clearly state what you desire. Your angels already know, but since they can't take away your free will, they wait patiently for us to make the first move.

A more formal way to ask for assistance is to find a quiet space in your home and dedicate it as a sacred space. You can create an altar featuring any (or all) of the following: images of angels, crystals, feathers, candles, or other meaningful objects.[11]

The altar can be small (like a shelf or windowsill) or even an entire room. Cleanse this area with sage regularly to allow you to connect more easily with your angels.

After grounding yourself and quieting your mind, feel free to light a candle or use roses to attract angels as they share the same frequency. Alternatively, you can use Angelite crystals, which are also known to attract angels due to their high vibration.

Remember, phrase it however you like. You can pray, talk informally, or even sing. Clearly communicate your intention.

For example, during a healing session, I said, "Archangel Raphael, Archangel Michael, guardian angels, ancestors, or spirit guides, please step forward and help me with this healing." My intention was to 'open, clear, balance & strengthen all energy points for her highest good.'

Next, close your eyes and breathe deeply several times to release any negative residue from the day.

Imagine being showered with sparkles of white light from heaven. Envision yourself receiving this beautiful and powerful energy that cleanses your troubled soul. Imagine their wings wrapped around you, shielding and releasing you from pain and unwanted memories.

You may feel this energy as pure love, experience warmth while sitting quietly, hear soft voices or thoughts that aren't yours, or feel a profound sense of calm.

When you want to end the connection, please take a moment to express gratitude for their presence.

In short, all you need to do is speak from your heart, be specific with your requests, pay attention to their answers, and create a consistent ritual.

There is no wrong way to do this, and the angels understand even if you forget something or it's messy and unpracticed. All they want is for you to give the green light by asking for their assistance.

What do you need help with?

Of course, when asking the Divine channel, your answers can show up in unexpected ways. Sometimes they do communicate through words (whether in your head, through a person, or a song), but often they use their own version of sign language.

Angelic Sign Language

Now that we know some of the basics of angels, let's go over the signs angels use to communicate with us. Remember that these signs could also be from a deceased loved one, ancestor, or pet who has crossed over the rainbow bridge.

When an angel is near, you may feel a cool breeze, an intense feeling of love, ringing in your ears, or tingling on the crown of your head. Sometimes my nose tickles persistently when angels want me to pay attention.

The first time it happened, I just signed up for the introductory college courses required for a degree in Social Work. My nose kept tickling for three days. Once I realized I had registered for the wrong math class, it stopped. Had I not changed classes, I would have been a year behind.

In the United States, the most well-known sign from an angel is when you see a cardinal. Your guardian angel may have prompted you to notice the red bird, and you automatically thought of someone in heaven.

Other common signs include finding pennies in unexpected places or finding a feather along your path. The sayings "pennies from heaven" and "when feathers appear, angels are near" are messages of love from heaven.

A rainbow symbolizes hope and peace. It's uplifting and encouraging, points to a bright future, and can symbolize making the right decision.

Angels may also communicate through scent.

Last week, I went to a restaurant with a friend. The place was fairly empty, so it was easy to find a seat. Then I suddenly smelled the scent of flowers, possibly roses. I thought it was the waitress's perfume, but my guest couldn't smell anything. Despite it being unexpected, I treasured the experience of an angelic visit during brunch.

Another way to receive a message is by daydreaming while gazing at the clouds. You may receive an answer to your question through a cloud formation.

One of my clients' dogs sent me a message in the form of her face in the clouds. She is a poodle with a distinctive-shaped head and ears, so I knew she was ready for another session. Sure enough, her mom confirmed this, saying, "Isabelle is bossy".

Pay attention to the music you listen to, as it may carry a message from your angels or deceased loved ones. Reflect on the memories they bring, especially if the song repeats.

While debating whether to submit an entry for a collaborative book, I soon received my answer after hearing the song "St. Elmo's Fire" each time I turned on the radio. This was the theme song for my college group of friends, as we constantly sought to uncover the meaning of life, much like the movie's characters.

A few days later, when I turned on the radio, I discovered that the radio station had shut down and was no longer available. This sign was my green light!

Since angels and our ancestors are energy, they can manipulate radios and electricity. Be mindful of flickering lights and consider your thoughts at the time this occurs. That helps determine who your visitor is and/or what they want to tell you.

Angels often reveal answers to your prayers through billboards, books, or license plates. You might wonder what the person's name was, and when you turn your head, you see the word 'Michael' on the side of a truck.

If you hear a phrase once, it's a conversation; if you hear it twice, pay attention; and if you hear it three times, it's a message from your angels.

Sometimes, a message can be a thought that pops into your head out of the blue, and you know it's a message because you never knew this information prior. Messages can come to you in your dreams, or you may see a sparkle of light, each color representing a different angel.

Archangel Michael is typically the first angel you will encounter, as he is the most well-known and their leader.

During COVID-19, I assisted my friend with her dog training business because it seemed that every family got a new puppy while stuck at home. I helped by conducting home visits to train their puppies. Sounds easy, right? Not for me. I always felt unsure of myself, even though I knew I needed to be more confident.

For the first 10 puppies I trained, I would sit in my car before approaching their front door and ask Archangel Michael to give me courage.

After my tenth request, I saw a flash of light in the shape of a human form, sparkling like fireworks! It rendered me speechless, yet I had to act normal since no one else had seen him. They reveal themselves when you least expect it.

Angel numerology is used as a sign from your angels, typically by repeatedly seeing triple digits. For example, you could see 111 three times in one day.

A book by Doreen Virtue defines the meaning of each number.[12] You can easily find interpretations of angel numbers online. 111 conveys that your thoughts manifest instantly, so keep them positive and allow fearful thoughts to be transformed. I tell my clients to make a wish at the precise moment they see this number.

These messages bring significant meaning into your life, reminding you that you'll never truly be alone.

It's essential to recognize that the first step toward healing is to move beyond survival mode, also known as the fight-or-flight stage. Once you start noticing angelic signs or messages, you'll connect to a whole new level of spirituality and heal your heart as the angels surround you with divine light and love.

My relationship with my angels began when I was newly divorced and living with several roommates in California. It was the most difficult time of my life, yet also the most amazing. After I moved in with a friend, I asked her about the clicking noises coming from my closet door. She smiled and said, "Oh, I get those too—it's the angels."

I wasn't prepared for that answer. Why would they be hanging around me in my room?

Then I realized they were always with me as I continued to hear the same tapping noises wherever I went. It still occurs today and has blossomed into a code system of communication. Another lightworker once told me that one click in your ear means yes, two means no. However, I've never heard of anyone else receiving this communication.

Your Angelic Support System

Before we conclude this chapter, I'd like to share some examples of my angelic support system in action from personal experience.

As a younger child, I often laid on my back looking at the ceiling before falling asleep, and observed a thin, white, cloud-like mist hovering over my bed. I had no idea what it was, but I was never afraid. Every time the yelling in the house upset me, the turmoil and fear would vanish once it came. This presence was my coping mechanism throughout childhood. I knew someone or something was watching over me, even though I didn't think it was my guardian angel!

I drew upon my faith in God's messengers to guide me as I grew older, especially after moving out of my childhood home. In my 30s, I never felt alone, even without a consistent family or many friends.

Once I became a social worker, there were numerous occasions when I found myself in unsafe situations. I entered homes known for domestic violence, witnessed a drug deal and an attempted shooting, and ensured my safety during a child removal situation. One family exhibited so much hostility toward me while at court that security escorted me in and out of the building.

Another family was in the witness protection program and feared the perpetrator knew their new address, so they sat on the floor to avoid being shot through the front window.

Tasked with keeping me safe, my guardian angel worked overtime right alongside me during all these times.

My angels were also highly protective of me when I lived alone in Cincinnati. After a night out, I asked my date to leave my apartment for the night, but he refused to budge. I started to panic. Suddenly, there was a loud ruffling noise from my kitchen, and he practically ran out the door.

My angel scared my date into leaving!

Apart from protecting you, they also guide you to find things beyond your wildest imagination.

For example, they guided me to find answers for a middle-aged lady who was diagnosed with Alzheimer's and was trying to qualify for assisted living through the Council on Aging®.

This visit fell to me because a co-worker called in sick again, and the home was far away from my territory, so I felt annoyed. However, as soon as I walked inside their house, an instant feeling of love surrounded me, and intuitively, I knew it was my client's guardian angels.

I walked in slow motion, and the sun shone brightly, or maybe it was the angels' glow. I said, "Your house is filled with angels!" There were too many to count.

My sense of self-esteem blossomed when I realized that our guardian angels see us as the most beautiful and precious beams of light and love. We're all part of God.

Discover how your angels can help navigate life's ups and downs.

Many Archangels would love to support your goals. Archangel Gabriel inspires creative writing and persuasive communication, Archangel Chamuel guides you to find a job you love, and Archangel Ariel lends a hand to open a business or transform your career.

Archangel Michael provides courage. Sometimes, even the smallest step can take an enormous amount of bravery. The first step can be the hardest. Once again, call on him for whatever scares you, such as public speaking, interviewing, meeting new friends, and having hard conversations.

Teaching others about angels is one of my passions, and I offer one-on-one spiritual mentorship to help you achieve your goals. Whatever you aim to accomplish can be done faster and more easily with an angelic support system.

Now you know who to ask for help, let's get your energy in the right place. In the next chapter, you'll learn how to maximize your energy and keep shining brightly, even when life mucks everything up.

CHAPTER 4

EVERYTHING IS ENERGY – 8 WAYS TO USE ENERGY FOR HEALING

Have you ever heard the following phrase stated by Pierre Teilhard de Chardin, *"I'm a spiritual being having a human experience?"*

Human beings came equipped with an energy system that we often take for granted. However, when it falls out of balance, it causes so much trouble that it becomes impossible to ignore.

We possess seven main chakras, or energy points, that align along our spine, as well as multiple meridians acting as pathways to distribute energy throughout our bodies. Additionally, we have an aura, a protective energy that surrounds our body with seven layers.

Do not overlook these chakras or aura, as they significantly influence our physical, emotional, and spiritual well-being.

THE 7 CHAKRAS

You have seven chakras, each associated with a color. These energy points correspond to a physical and emotional attribute of your body.

White – The Crown Chakra

The white crown chakra influences how you perceive the world around you and is connected to your spirituality. Some people will never have an open Crown Chakra if they haven't spiritually evolved, or if they feel stuck in life.

When it's blocked or in overdrive, it can cause all sorts of havoc.

Physical issues when blocked:

- Migraines
- Insomnia or sleep issues
- Problems with your nervous system
- Brain tumours

Emotional issues when blocked:

- Struggling with finding your purpose
- Feeling disconnected from reality
- Anxiety (overthinking)
- Inability to focus
- Materialistic
- Making ego-based decisions
- Addicted to spirituality

Benefits of a healthy Crown Chakra:

- ❖ Clarity
- ❖ Wisdom
- ❖ Enlightenment
- ❖ Spiritual Connection
- ❖ Lasting Happiness

Indigo – The Third Eye Chakra

The indigo Third Eye Chakra helps you see where you're going in life and how to get there. With it, you see beyond the present and the physical, to avoid deception or missteps.

Physical issues when blocked:
- Headaches
- Vision problems
- Ear and/or nose problems
- Hallucinations
- Nightmares

Emotional issues when blocked:
- Obsessing over people or material objects
- Mental confusion
- Lack of focus
- Uncoordinated

Benefits of a healthy Third Eye Chakra:
- ❖ Fully developed intuition
- ❖ Divinely Creative
- ❖ Mental clarity
- ❖ Laser-focused
- ❖ Easily make decisions

Blue – The Throat Chakra

The blue Throat Chakra allows you to communicate your desires and needs and speak up for yourself. You use this chakra to connect to loved ones and resolve conflicts.

Physical issues when blocked:
- Weak voice

- Neck issues
- TMJ and jaw problems

Emotional issues when blocked:
- Trouble listening
- Can't express needs
- Shyness
- Talking too much or too little
- Misunderstanding/ gossiping
- Disengages from or interrupts conversations

Benefits of a healthy Throat Chakra:
- ❖ Confidently communicate
- ❖ Express your needs clearly
- ❖ Good listener
- ❖ People listen to what you have to say

Green – The Heart Chakra

The state of your green Heart Chakra indicates if you're able to give or receive love. You need it to connect with others and let people in.

Physical issues when blocked:
- Lung problems
- Heart problems
- Asthma
- Low immunity

Emotional issues when blocked:
- Jealous
- Depressed
- Lonely
- Self-centered
- Lack of empathy

- No self-love

Benefits of a healthy Heart Chakra:
- Able to give love freely
- Able to receive love freely
- Love yourself
- Independent
- Feeling fulfilled
- Able to trust
- Compassionate

Yellow – The Solar Plexus Chakra

The yellow Solar Plexus Chakra influences your confidence, allowing you to be optimistic and to keep going even when facing obstacles.

Physical issues when blocked:
- Eating disorders
- Digestive problems
- Pancreas issues
- Stomach and gallbladder problems
- Always tired

Emotional issues when blocked:
- Low self-esteem
- No self-control
- Unreliable
- No sense of humour
- Bravado, outbursts of aggression
- Lack of confidence in others

Benefits of a healthy Solar Plexus Chakra:
- Optimistic and positive
- High self-esteem
- Confident in life and others

- ❖ Full of energy
- ❖ Reliable
- ❖ Able to have fun even in serious situations
- ❖ Easily spot the silver lining

Orange – The Sacral Chakra

The orange Sacral Chakra fuels your creativity, allows you to enjoy life, and sensualizes your sexuality. Without it, you simply exist without feeling much of anything.

Physical issues when blocked:
- Reproductive problems
- Sexual dysfunction (sex addiction when in overdrive)
- Lower back pain
- Urinary tract issues
- Blood sugar problems
- Addictions

Emotional issues when blocked:
- Feeling numb
- Overreacting to things
- Emotionally dependent
- Deny pleasure
- No desires or passions

Benefits of a healthy Sacral Chakra:
- ❖ Creative
- ❖ Able to enjoy life
- ❖ Enjoy sensuality and sexuality
- ❖ Find your passion
- ❖ Emotionally balanced
- ❖ Able to feel freely

Red – The Root Chakra

The red root chakra supports you like the roots of a tree. It grounds your energy, making you feel safe and supported.

Physical issues when blocked:
- Leg and knee problems
- Issues with your feet
- Pain in the tailbone
- Sluggish

Emotional issues when blocked:
- Feeling anxious or unsafe
- Ungrounded
- Hard to concentrate
- Feeling like you don't belong
- Not open to change
- Lazy (avoiding scary things)
- In fight or flight mode

Benefits of a healthy Root Chakra:
- Feel like you belong
- Safe and secure
- Confident and grounded
- Able to concentrate
- Easily weather even life's roughest storms

If your body is misaligned, one or more of your chakras will be closed, and your emotions will be affected. This blocked chakra remains that way for years if you let it, which is when diseases can develop.

By unblocking all chakras, your energy will flow evenly and strongly throughout your body.

These chakras open and close independently, but we can make them stay open by raising our vibration (as discussed in Chapter 2) or by maintaining good health.

Additionally, we have layers of energy surrounding our bodies that can develop tears or holes, allowing negative energy to enter our aura. The colors that characterize a healthy aura can also indicate physical and emotional well-being.

Below is a chart comparing healthy and unhealthy auras. If it becomes damaged or affected in any way, it will shift to darker colors and sometimes even black.

Each layer indicates the health of your energy.

Etheric Layer: Closest to the body, reflects physical health.

Emotional Layer: Manages emotions and feelings.

Mental Layer: Governs thoughts and cognitive processes.

Astral Layer: Connects to the heart and relationships.

Etheric Layer: Contains the blueprint for the physical body.

Celestial Layer: Reflects spiritual awareness and enlightenment.

Causal Layer: The outermost layer, connecting to infinite consciousness.

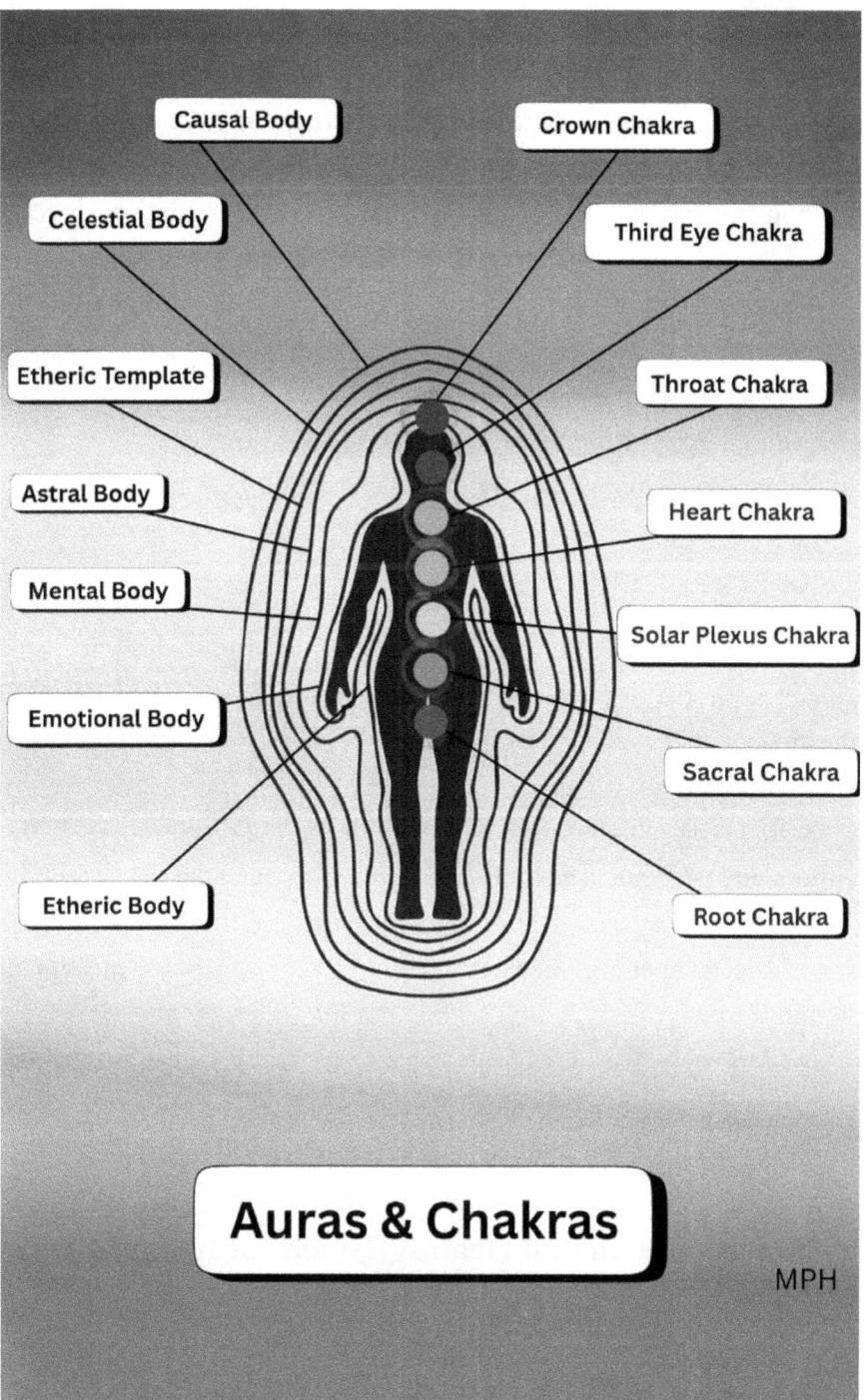

The chart above illustrates a healthy energy system, displaying the chakras and aura.

You may wonder how to heal your energy and open your chakras. You can balance your chakras through meditation, practicing yoga, reciting mantras, tapping, using essential oils, engaging in breathwork, sound therapy, and connecting with nature.

These modalities are holistic and used in conjunction with mainstream medicine. They support four key levels: mental, emotional, physical, and spiritual. Used well, they release stuck, blocked, and stagnant energy (including trauma).

Below, you'll find eight ways to use energy for healing.

1. Reiki

Reiki is the most common and oldest form of energy healing. Its name comes from the Japanese words "rei," meaning universal, and "ki," meaning vital life force energy (more literally, it translates to spirit, energy, or power).

Reiki involves the transfer of energy through a practitioner's palms, either above the body or by laying hands on your fully clothed body. The recipient may experience a tingling sensation. Results can manifest as a release, an opening, deep healing, or a flow of energy and movement within the body.

It offers deep relaxation, clears stagnant energy, balances the chakras, alleviates pain and depression, releases mental fatigue and stress, promotes healing from trauma, and ultimately provides peace.

2. Healing Touch and Healing Touch for Animals©

The primary difference between Reiki and Healing Touch is the emphasis that Healing Touch places on intention, which refers to the practitioner's desired outcome. For example, healers may ask specifically to balance, open, clear, and strengthen all energy points for their client's highest good.

Additionally, the energy from Healing Touch and Healing Touch for Animals© is channeled from Heaven, God, or the Angels, making the practitioner's body a vessel to promote healing. Reiki's energy draws from universal energy.

Another distinction is that Healing Touch practitioners assess the chakras before and after the session, typically using a pendulum and hand movements over the body. Healing Touch requires learning many techniques, whereas Reiki relies on energy flowing where it's needed. Both therapies are highly beneficial, whether provided in person or remotely.

Carol Komitor, a former veterinary technician, founded Healing Touch for Animals®, an energy therapy program for animals, because she discovered people didn't understand the differences in the energy system between humans and animals.

So, how does this healing affect an animal's body?

The energy therapy initiates relaxation, releasing endorphins and toxins, while it relaxes the muscles. It increases circulation and oxygen levels, builds enzymes for proper digestion, regulates hormones, and healthy cells begin to regenerate. While promoting healing, it also helps regulate the immune system.

I didn't realize how life-changing and profound this work would be until my first healing session as a volunteer at the SPCA. There was a white and pink pitbull who couldn't sit on her right hip due to an injury. A few days passed as she waited for her appointment with the vet.

Since she showed me her teeth as she barked, I was a bit frightened to go inside her kennel.

Calmly, I sat down next to her and did a projected healing session specifically on her hip to help with the pain. Prior to this, she shook with fear, and I consoled her with a soothing voice.

After about twenty minutes, she could sit comfortably on both hips!

I was so touched when her blue eyes locked with mine. For a moment, we truly connected. She sent me lots of love while licking my face, neck, and arms. At that moment, I was hooked and couldn't wait to help more animals!

Volunteering at the SPCA allowed me to learn the best techniques for rescue animals while obtaining my Certification.

An Advanced Proficiency technique with Healing Touch, that works for both humans and animals suffering from PTSD, is called The Amygdala Trauma Release.

The practitioner activates the amygdala, a brain structure that regulates emotions, and applies this to their adrenal system and throughout the body. This activation helps bring the human or pet back into a safe state, rather than remaining in a state of fight, flight, or freeze.

Each case is unique, depending on the severity of the trauma for pets or humans. However, I helped several individuals release severe recurring nightmares.

More specifically, I conducted two separate remote sessions for two teenage brothers who experienced abuse and neglect and witnessed violence starting at the ages of four and six. The mom and grandmother tried for almost six years to help their children acclimate back into society without success.

The youngest child, Dwaine, a twelve-year-old, got results quickly. His anger decreased, along with the time needed to put him to bed. Before, it would take 3-4 hours for him to go to sleep because he was terrified (the abuse would occur in the evening while sleeping). His mom reported that he no longer suffers from nightmares. Dwaine now sleeps through the night and wakes up with a smile. He said that during the session, he felt lighter and less stiff, and could feel it working.

A few days later, for the first time in years, he allowed his mom to hug him.

The older brother, Ray, a fourteen-year-old, did well too, until he got triggered and reverted to fight-or-flight mode. That said, Ray endured twice as much abuse as his brother and is still learning how to control his triggers. Overall, this technique is a game-changer for anyone experiencing PTSD symptoms, whether child, adult, or pet.

Another interesting scenario happened when I helped a six-month-old puppy that appeared to be in pain. The vet agreed there was pain, although he referred the owner to a neurologist.

The owners decided to call me instead, as I had helped them with another pet of theirs.

As it turns out, the puppy was absorbing the owner's pain from a recent back surgery. I pinpointed the exact vertebrae causing the pain. Once I released the stuck energy, he was his playful puppy self again!

With animal communication, I told the puppy to be a loving companion only and not absorb his owner's pain. The owners were delighted to have their fun-loving puppy back to normal, and they thanked me repeatedly. Knowing that I made a positive impact on their lives made it worthwhile.

3. Acupuncture

Acupuncture manipulates a person's energy system by using thin needles strategically placed at specific points in the body.

It provides comfort related to various diseases, including (but not limited to) chemotherapy-induced and postoperative nausea and vomiting, dental pain, fibromyalgia, headaches, labor pain, lower back pain, neck pain, osteoarthritis, menstrual cramps, allergies, and tennis elbow.

Most importantly, acupuncture is an effective treatment option for PTSD, offering a holistic approach to managing both the mental and physical repercussions of traumatic events. Its ability to regulate the nervous system and alleviate symptoms such as anxiety, depression, and chronic pain, positions it as an invaluable first-line treatment for PTSD.

4. Integrated Energy Therapy

Integrated Energy Therapy is possibly the least known holistic modality. What is IET? It is a powerful technique that helps get the 'issues out of your tissues'.

Developed by Stevan J. Thayer, a former Bell Laboratories engineer, IET utilizes the violet energy ray to work directly with your 12-strand spiritual DNA. IET supports you in safely and gently releasing limiting energy patterns from your past, empowering and balancing your life in the present, and helping you reach for the stars as you evolve into your future.

Its founder states: "We chose the term 'Integrated' in our name to convey our vision of integrating past experiences into the power of the present to bring about the joy of the future. The IET Mission is to 'Heal the world one heart at a time'."

This modality works directly with the Archangels, who allow the healer to help our DNA system erase past trauma or limiting belief systems.

A practitioner must be 'attuned' by an IET Master Instructor to be considered a practitioner. This modality can be combined with Healing Touch sessions to incorporate angelic assistance.

5. Mediumship

There are three additional ways to heal trauma with energy. I include mediumship, which is particularly useful when addressing generational trauma. This decision comes from firsthand experience with a medium who helped me understand the family dynamics of my past generations.

A medium also introduced me to my Spirit Guide, my deceased grandfather, whom I never met on Earth. I discovered that he shares the same healing abilities as I do and that he guides me to excel in my profession as a healer.

Additionally, it's beneficial to seek guidance from our ancestors. Knowing the past helps you avoid making the same mistake in the present. When a medium reaches them, they often convey how loved and protected you truly are now.

6. Sound Healing

Sound healing can break up energetic congestion, balance your chakras, provide grounding and harmony, and deepen relaxation.

When using music as a way of healing, it must have the frequency of the pure fifth interval (200 Hz) and a second tone with a frequency of 300 Hz. Some CDs offering this frequency are used for meditation or as background music.

Another way is to use Pair 5 tuning forks. Those are the fifth and sixth forks in the series of thirteen forks developed by INNER SOUND. Each tuning fork vibrates at a different frequency. Tap them on rubber and put them close to your ears to experience the effects.

I use mine as a quick way to balance my chakras and become more grounded.

7. Vibrational Healing

Vibrational healing can be applied directly to people or pets, positioning the tuning fork or OM Turner directly on the area of discomfort. It requires holding the fork at the bottom so it can vibrate directly into the body, releasing pain and stuck energy.

I've used my tuning forks to release tension in my jaws and my OM Turner to release pain from a pet's back.

A way to incorporate both sound and vibrational therapy is by attending a Sound Bath or a Singing Bowl session, which also incorporates chimes, bells, a rain stick, and Tibetan or crystal bowls. Your body releases the muck through the vibrations of the music.

If it's your first session, the instructor will encourage you to monitor your body for any uncomfortable palpitations.

When I attended my first session, my heartbeat increased threefold, and I feared I was having a heart attack or that my heart might explode. This sensation lasted for 30 minutes of the 45-minute session.

After it was over, I asked the instructor about its cause, and she explained that the combination of sound and vibration was healing my heart chakra by releasing trapped emotions. My first time was intense, but it was well worth the experience.

The intensity depends on how much stuck energy you need to release and how easily you release it. For you, it might be a slow process, clearing up a little more each time.

8. Pet's Energy

Another way to use energy for healing is to connect with your pet or farm animal's energy. They already know your feelings, thoughts, and behaviors, making it easy to create a link.

For instance, horses use their loving energy to help their owners overcome traumatic events. Their energy is bigger than a football field, their frequency is five times greater than yours, and their heart is ten times larger than yours. This energy expands and opens your heart.

As powerful yet sensitive creatures, they teach humans about love, trust, and self-confidence. Being with them lowers your heart rate and blood pressure, while reducing stress hormones known as cortisol.

Additionally, time spent in nature helps keep you grounded and at peace.

Many people with a PTSD diagnosis use equine therapy to help them process their emotions through the horse's energy. The individual can't hide their feelings from the horse, because the animal already knows their state of mind. A horse can feel a human's heartbeat from four feet away. Eventually, the horse synchronizes its heart with ours, which helps us stay calm and regulate our nervous system.

Cats are known to be mystical, psychic, and very intuitive.

They provide vibrational healing through the frequency of their purring, which is at 25 to 150 Hertz. Their purring helps humans breathe more easily, promotes self-soothing, and regulates pain and inflammation. Additionally, it produces endorphins within the brain, which promote relaxation. They use this frequency to help heal their owners from various physical and mental ailments.

A study published in *Medical News Today* found that cat owners are 40% less likely to have a heart attack, as pets can help lower blood pressure, relieve stress, assist with shortness of breath, alleviate migraines, and decrease pain.[13] Additionally, they can assist their owners in healing from wounds and injuries to muscles, tendons, and ligaments.

A cat's saliva has anti-bacterial properties used to clean themselves and heal any physical wounds. They can help you recover from a scratch faster with their saliva.

Don't be surprised if your cat wants to lie on the injured area of your body, as their vibration helps you to heal and soothe pain.

Cats have a keen sense of smell and detect hormones related to various diagnoses such as cancer, diabetes, depression, and even pregnancy. Additionally, they know when someone is dying, as they can sense the changes in a person's pheromones and body chemistry.

Research confirmed that stroking a cat causes a release of the "love hormone" in humans. The technical term for this neurochemical is oxytocin, a hormone released when people fall in love. Oxytocin increases your emotional perception!

Have you ever heard someone say, 'Cats are like walking crystals'?

It's true. According to the NIH, the National Institute of Health, cats have calcite crystals in their pineal gland that can transmute energy from negative to positive. They will sit in areas that need cleansing, and they can discern between good and evil spirits. They are our protectors from the spirit world, and can see what is invisible to us.

Just like cats, dogs help lower blood pressure and stress, and also possess a keen sense of smell that can detect different diseases.

However, dogs improve our cardiovascular health by providing regular walks. Dogs also offer a social connection, allowing owners to meet neighbors while walking, visit dog parks, or attend dog-related events. These outings alleviate loneliness.

Known to provide comfort to humans, dogs intuitively sense when someone needs more attention than others.

A nearby police station has a therapy dog for their precinct to help the police officers process the trauma they experience. If they have a bad day, they get showered with unconditional love through licks and kisses. Some retirement homes allow visits from social companion dogs to help residents feel less alone.

As you can see, all eight of these modalities provide trauma release physically, emotionally, spiritually, or mentally. Next, we will look into some tips and tools to help heal your trauma that have already worked for me and many of my clients.

CHAPTER 5

10 Spiritual Tools for Trauma Healing

The spiritual tools in this chapter will help you maintain your energy at its fullest potential, assist in healing your trauma, and keep you at a higher frequency. They will also support you in focusing on present-moment activities, practicing mindfulness, and fostering self-love.

Keep in mind that these are tools and not a substitute for other professional help, such as a psychiatrist, psychologist, licensed social worker, or case manager. Use them in conjunction with traditional mental health treatment.

Let's go over each of the ten tools.

1. ESSENTIAL OILS

Aromatherapy is one of the simplest ways to elevate your vibration. Essential oils are extracted from the most concentrated essence of trees, fruits, herbs, grasses, shrubs, or flowers. Each oil possesses its own energetic frequency.

Rose oil has the highest frequency at 320 MHz, followed by frankincense (147 MHz), lavender (118 MHz), and myrrh (105 MHz). Angels are drawn to roses because they vibrate at a similar level.

Aromatherapy stimulates the olfactory receptors in the nose, sending signals to the brain's limbic system, which is responsible for emotions, memory, and other cognitive functions.

This stimulation elicits various physical and emotional responses, such as relaxation, stress reduction, and an improved mood. Essential oils offer numerous additional health benefits like improved memory, pain management, reduced inflammation, enhanced skin health, boosted immunity, and relief from respiratory issues.

Essential oils can be inhaled directly, infused, used topically, or ingested.

To use them safely, it's important to use a carrier oil such as Coconut, Olive, Sunflower, Jojoba, Argan, or Rosehip oil. Like essential oils, flower essences, such as Bach Original Flower Remedies®, can be used to support moods, alleviate anxiety, and reduce worry.

There are some guidelines to follow when using essential oils around or on pets. For instance, when diffusing with a carrier oil, Tea Tree Oil should never be used around or directly on cats, as this oil is considered toxic.

First, let your pet smell the essential oil to determine if they like the scent. Don't try to force them or administer it internally; always dilute it with a safe carrier oil. Some essential oils you should never use on a cat, like oregano, wintergreen, clove, peppermint, and thyme.

Additionally, when applying oil to a cat, put it behind their neck to prevent them from licking it.

Dogs and horses are somewhat more tolerant of essential oils. However, it's still important to follow the guidelines provided by Young Living Essential Oils® for all animals. They offer pre-diluted essential oils specifically formulated for pets, and Bach Original Flower Remedies has options designed to assist anxious or stressed pets.

2. PROTECTING YOUR ENERGY

One crucial spiritual practice is to learn how to protect your high-frequency energy from energy vampires, also known as narcissists. Your energy will stand out to them since they depleted theirs. Walking in darkness, your light draws them in.

They don't want to do the work because it's all about what they can gain from others. Manipulating empaths is a sport to them, and they think your bleeding heart makes you easy to control. The strengths of empaths (sympathizing and caring) become weaknesses when faced with these individuals.

It can be difficult to cut these people off, especially when they're family or loved ones. Circumstances can make things especially complicated, like in the case of Mary Jane.

Mary Jane and Simon dated for six months until tragedy struck. She was hit by a vehicle in a crosswalk on her way to meet him for dinner. After being in a coma for several months, doctors feared the worst. But she pulled through.

Simon visited her every day and agreed to be her caregiver while she recovered.

Fast forward three years, he constantly put her down for things she couldn't do, made everything her fault, and took advantage of her memory loss. He made her feel like she was going crazy. Angry and depressed, he complained about how much he had to endure.

While Mary Jane was physically doing better, she suffered from short-term memory loss and couldn't hold down a job. Her boyfriend stopped talking to her and would leave her for hours at a time while he drank and golfed with his buddies.

One morning, she had a seizure, but no one noticed. Simon left without checking on her, so she remained in bed when she should have been at work. Mary Jane's boss left at least eight voicemails for Simon, asking for news. Calls left unanswered, her boss sent the police to do a safety check. That's when Mary Jane realized she couldn't remember the past two days.

Officially diagnosed with amnesia, her doctor reiterated that she needed a caregiver. She couldn't drive, walk steadily, or even remember to take her medications.

Simon turned up the charm, promising to supervise her as he worked from home. Once home, the emotional abuse continued. Then he left for a week on vacation. In front of Mary Jane's family, he acted like a loving boyfriend.

These kinds of people specialize in temporarily showing you or your family a 'good side'. Because it's not genuine, they can't maintain it for long, but they call on it systematically to make you remember how good it once was and long for even a sliver of hope that it will be that way again. That's how they keep you hooked. Then, they make you feel bad for not sympathizing with their situation and even considering leaving them.

The following technique works whether you just met an energy vampire or you've had one around you for quite some time. It's time to stop giving them your energy.

Visualize a light pink bubble around your body or mirrors flashing outward for protection. The negative energy bounces off and returns to the sender. Don't hesitate to call on Archangel Michael to lend a hand if you feel you're not strong enough.

One person I know energetically extracts herself from the situation by saying, 'Beam me up,' like on Star Trek.

There are many ways to do this. There is no right or wrong, only what feels right to you. You can choose something with a special meaning to you, to make it easier to remember when you feel distressed. You can also carry crystals, which we'll discuss next, to have a physical item to hold when in need of protection.

Make sure you protect your animals as well.

According to Psychology Today, narcissists who own pets treat them as an extension of themselves, as it will enhance their image and ego. They will spoil them, talk to them in public, and use them for attention-seeking. At times, they use the pet as an excuse to not socialize or make their partners jealous. They may pay more attention to the pet than the human or hold the pet hostage during a divorce agreement.

In contrast, a narcissist may start to neglect their pet if it's no longer getting them enough attention and isn't useful anymore. This disinterest could turn into abuse because they don't have empathy for anyone, including animals.

3. CRYSTALS

There are several ways to protect yourself and your pets. I believe that every empath should wear or carry a Black Onyx, Black Tourmaline, or Black Obsidian. These three crystals will block psychic attacks, protect energy, and transmute negative energy into positive energy.

For grounding, choose a Red Jasper or a Smoky Quartz crystal.

Amethyst helps you relax and balance your moods. So when my husband wasn't sleeping through the night, I put an amethyst crystal candle holder under the bed, and he slept like a cat in its favorite basket!

In Chapter 2, I mentioned David Vogel crystals, which offer the same protection and can amplify good energy during meditation. When using the female side, the crystal is elevated and has a point to receive energy. The male side is flat to block energy.

Also, Etsy sells crystals that clip onto a pet's collar to protect their energy, help them stay grounded, or open a specific chakra.

If there's an area where they sleep, you can place a rose quartz near them on a shelf to fill the room with love. However, never put a crystal inside their bed. It would be too easy and tempting for them to swallow it.

Here are several ways to cleanse your crystals:
- Place them outside or on a windowsill under a full moon or in direct sunlight while soaking them in holy water for extra protection.
- Sage your crystals to clear negative energy.
- Make your own saltwater and soak the crystals for 2-4 minutes (rinse them thoroughly afterward).
- Wash them in rainwater.
- Use a charging plate made out of selenite crystal to cleanse your smaller crystals by placing them on the plate. (Remember that selenite shouldn't get wet and doesn't require cleansing.)

4. CLEANSING YOUR ENERGY

Did you know that shaking someone's hand transfers your energy to them and vice versa? Some people are unaware of this and wonder why they feel drained after interacting with a person of low vibrational energy. The following image illustrates this transfer perfectly.

Energy Transference

An example of a friend shaking your hand who is in emotional distress. They talk to you about how upset they are while your energy is absorbing their energy. You are left feeling drained, and they walk away feeling better.

MPH

Your environment also affects your energy, in more ways and to a greater extent than you may think.

My friend and I went into a new metaphysical store and immediately felt unsettled and lightheaded. Granted, it was an old house; however, the items in their store were on what I call the 'witchy' side. Head throbbing, it became hard to breathe. My friend was in a similar state.

We walked upstairs to the room designated for a group meditation. The black painted walls matched the curtains, and people wore long black dresses.

We glanced at each other, then left without explanation, rushing downstairs to get outside so we could breathe a little better.

In contrast, I entered several different rooms set up for Singing Bowl sessions and immediately felt lighter. Those places always felt comfortable and safe, with a welcoming feeling. Most practitioners clear their room before events with sage and crystals.

Learning how to cleanse your energy is essential.

You can practice dry bathing (think of it like energetically wiping yourself down) after being in public, large crowds, intense situations, or around intense people. This type of bathing involves using a selenite wand or your hands to sweep energy off your body, cleansing your aura. The crystal will absorb this energy. If you're using your hands, flick all five fingers at the end to expel the energy.

Another option is to use sage to cleanse your aura, which clears negative energy, and palo santo wood to bring in positive energy.

Sage your pet if they've been out in public with you or even at daycare. They're empaths too, and absorb other people's emotions. Pets have pixels instead of auras, but you cleanse their energy field the same way.

My favorite practice is taking a spiritual shower, visualizing a white light flowing from heaven to cleanse my aura with beautiful sparkles of love.

Additionally, a lovely way to cleanse my space or home is by using rose water with a rose quartz crystal, which charges the water and infuses it with love and positivity. Placing rose quartz in the corners of each room raises the vibration to the frequency of love.

You may wonder why this is important.

These are ways to raise your vibration, as we discussed before. You can change your lifestyle and feel calmer knowing you aren't holding onto anyone else's energy but your own.

Your perspective shifts when you realize that everything (even our words, thoughts, and actions) is energy, because you're a spiritual being experiencing a human body. Awareness of your vibration helps you gauge your emotions and take care of your health on a physical, mental, emotional, and spiritual level.

5. PENDULUM

As a healer, I use my pendulum almost daily to answer yes-or-no questions to see if the chakras are open or closed. The answers appear through the energy of the pendulum as it swings in one of two different directions, depending on the answer.

Before using your new pendulum, you must program it by stating, "Show me what the answer Yes looks like." Then, "Show me what the answer No looks like." The answers will always be in two different directions and will remain this way.

Most of my pendulums are crystals. However, artisans can also make them from copper, wood, or steel. It's essential to cleanse them regularly, as they will break if you don't clear them of negative energy.

You'll be surprised by what you can discover with a pendulum. One time, before the Cincinnati Bengals' Super Bowl game, I asked my pendulum if the Bengals would win. It said no. Nobody from the group

I was with wanted to hear this, so I immediately played it down like it wasn't true.

Sure enough, the Bengals lost within the last few seconds of overtime.

6. THE MOON

Another tool is to align your goals with the moon cycles to stay on track. Many cultures hold full moon ceremonies to honor the moon's power, and it's considered the best time to manifest your dreams.

The New Moon cultivates new beginnings, so start on a New Moon. Rest, reflect, and plan what you would like to accomplish that month.

Then, during the First Quarter, work on your projects, adjusting as needed to complete them by the full moon.

On the Full Moon, you put your projects out into the world, which is why it's called manifesting. At the same time, during the Full Moon, you release what is no longer needed to move forward to the Third Quarter, where you wrap up any loose ends.

Cleanse your crystals on a full moon, and cleanse yourself mentally and physically. Take an Epsom salt bath (highly recommended) to release toxins from your body and allow your system to absorb the magnesium for stress relief. Then, mentally, release negative thoughts and behaviors that no longer serve you.

You may notice it's a full moon if your pet has the zoomies. They might overreact, or bark, meow, or neigh more frequently than usual, as they intuitively release energy too. Pets, just like people, are affected by the moon's energy.

If you miss the exact date, the same energy becomes active three days before the full moon and remains active three days after. During the completion phase of the full moon, decide which negative feelings, thoughts, or behaviors you'd like to let go of that no longer serve you. Meditate to help you release these patterns.

Then you're back to a New Moon to start all over again.

7. MANIFESTING

In 2009, Oprah Winfrey invited the author of 'The Secret' to her talk show, and the world went crazy over this book and short film. It has been translated into over 50 languages and has sold over 30 million copies.

Today, The Secret is better known as The Law of Attraction, where you manifest your wishes through visualization and positive thoughts. You believe them into existence. Dr. Wayne Dyer's book, 'Manifest Your Destiny: Nine Spiritual Principles for Getting Everything You Want,' is another excellent resource.

Manifesting isn't just about positive thinking and ignoring the possibility of failure.

It goes beyond maintaining a positive mindset and focusing on what you want rather than what you don't want. You need to live the experience as if it were already happening and take concrete actions in the real world to make space for your desired outcome (like making room in a cabinet), without being attached to *how* it unfolds.

For example, when you say 'I'll only accept money if I earn it myself', you block money in other forms, such as an unexpected gift or tax return.

One way I manifest is through repeating positive affirmations throughout the day for about a week. One in particular is, "I'm open to receiving abundance in every area of my life." It makes me feel hopeful and excited!

When I did this the other day, I received many unexpected clients, compliments, and business connections. Also, I received small surprises such as my husband making a bouquet for me at work while landscaping, a check in the mail from a rebate I'd forgotten about, and a care package from a friend while I was sick.

My friend's daughter, Lauren, who is getting married in November, manifested her relationship this way.

Her motto is Ask, Believe, and Receive!

However, she took it one step further with her actions, as she bought two of everything she needed for her new apartment, so that they could share them after they met. Additionally, to attract a masculine energy, she purchased men's cologne. Her actions showed the Universe that she was serious and ready. In the meantime, she acted as if her wish had already come true.

Patience and clarity are key when it comes to manifesting.

She made a seemingly impossible list of all her wishes, and though it was a tall order, she got it all and then some!

She actively prayed each day for this relationship for over two years. It almost became a joke when she asked God, "And by the way, can you make sure he knows how to cook and has blue eyes?"

God always responded to her by saying, "Don't worry about it! I've got this. Live your life and chill!" So she did, and didn't actively pursue a relationship, as she sensed that he would come to her when she least expected it.

In the meantime, I had no idea that she had been manifesting a relationship, as we only met once.

The surprise ending is that I introduced her to her Prince Charming! I'm considered her Fairy Godmother and will officially be a part of the family.

It was so unexpected. I met him at our local winery. In a very friendly atmosphere, we all talked openly. He shared that he lived down the street and was going through a horrific divorce.

After meeting him about three times, it hit me as we talked. I need to set him up with someone. I couldn't let a good man go to waste! While thinking this, I mentally went through a list of my friends, trying to figure out how old he was and who I knew around his age.

Suddenly, Lauren's name popped into my mind.

I immediately found her picture on Facebook to show him and to see if he would be interested. "Isn't she beautiful?"

He froze, and his mouth fell open in disbelief! "Yes, she is beautiful!"

I made arrangements for her mom to meet him at the winery, since that was where we would go anyway to hang out. After meeting him, she practically cried when she realized what a perfect match he would be for her daughter. The following week, we made up an excuse for Lauren to come to the winery, and the rest is history!

They immediately clicked and started dating exclusively from that day forward.

Lauren said that he loves the coffee cup she picked out for him years ago, and still uses it to this day. He used to be a professional chef, so he's an excellent cook. Their religious beliefs aligned. He is tall, dark, and handsome, with blue eyes. Additionally, he has two children, which Lauren considered a huge bonus!

Her grandma prayed for her over the years as well, but to St Joseph. One of the first times Lauren was in her fiancé's home, she saw a prayer card of St. Joseph on his desk! As they got to know each other, they discovered many coincidences and serendipities, and soon realized that they were meant to be together forever. It was kismet.

It has been a fairy tale come true for both, and I can't wait for their wedding. All because she never gave up, believed it would happen, and was ready for him when the time finally came.

Keep on believing in miracles, because they happen every day!

8. MEDITATION

When you meditate, you'll need to ground yourself. To do this, direct all your energy to your feet and calm your emotions through deep breathing. You'll feel free from stress in the present moment, which helps you focus on your goals for the month.

There are several ways to meditate, and it doesn't always need to be on a full moon.

Most people think of meditation as sitting in silence quietly, cross-legged, and with their pinkies out. This method is only one of many approaches, and it takes practice to entirely still your thoughts and sit in a meditative state.

If it doesn't fit your lifestyle, you can meditate while exercising, doing the dishes, or even bathing.

We tend to turn our thoughts off while performing mundane day-to-day tasks. I receive messages from my angels when I'm in water, whether it's taking a bath, shower, jacuzzi, or swimming.

You can listen to a guided meditation, in which the narrator guides you to release stuck energy, relax each muscle to achieve total relaxation, balance your chakras, ask for protection, or receive divine intervention from the archangels.

Always leave your door open at home when you meditate so your pet, especially your cats, can join you.

They sense the vibrations of the calming energy produced during meditation, and love it when we have a clear mind because it makes it easier for them to relax as well.

I learned a healing modality for pets called The Trust Technique, which enables you to help your pet with behavioral problems by silencing your mind and meditating. This approach fosters a strong bond between humans and animals, allowing them to lower their guard and trust again.

Some meditations specialize in helping you cut energetic cords.

These cords are invisible energetic connections between people, which also explains telepathy. Constantly staying connected drains your battery. Connections can be positive, toxic, or neutral (which no longer serve you).

Toxic energy is harder to cut off because, unlike passive neutral connections, the person it belongs to refuses to let go of their personal battery. When faced with toxic energy, ask Archangel Michael to use his sword to cut these connections to free you from this person's energy.

I repeated this process with my mother several times. Even though we haven't seen each other for over 25 years, I could still feel her negative energy each time she tried to reconnect.

The disconnected person will feel an energetic void and a sense of loss even before they realize you've physically cut them off as well. Then the person will reach out to you and try to convince you to return to their life, or perhaps invent a reason to reconnect. Keep your boundaries.

9. FOCUS LIFE-FORCE ENERGY

What if you could live in a higher level of consciousness without even trying to raise your vibration? In an environment where everyone is friendlier to each other, even when they don't get along?

Imagine experiencing the same benefits as visiting Machu Picchu, one of the World's Seven Wonders, which radiates high vibrational energy, while sitting on your couch.

This program offers Chi Life Force Energy, providing 24 hours a day of unconditional love.

The program, known as Focus Life-Force Energy (FLFE), provides energy to connect to a specific address, such as your home or business, your phone, jewelry, or even a water bottle. The FLFE machine is similar to Nikola Tesla's in that it uses stacks of plates and coils to provide quantum standing waves.

Someone who became severely ill due to the multiple 5G cell towers in Florida referred me to this program.

She relocated to decrease the side effects from EMF as she's hypersensitive to this type of radiation, and her cats suffered from it as well. This program helped her recover, along with multiple other modalities and treatments.

After a two-week trial, I was hooked. It helped me increase the outcomes of my energy sessions with animals!

As a practitioner, I must maintain a high vibration to be an effective healer. When I added FLFE to my home, I noticed a significant difference in the quality of my distance sessions. My ability to sense energy increased, along with the tingling in my hands, which indicates that the movement of energy is strongly shifting to balance the chakras.

I noticed that the energy in my home lightened because it vibrated at 650, which is associated with peace and love.

This higher energy supports positivity, mental clarity, increased memory, positive habits, and better emotional regulation. Even my pets were calmer and extra loving.

Furthermore, it creates an optimal environment to release trauma without requiring any additional support. It helps you remain present, explore shadow work, and boost your self-love, while also aiding your physical healing process.

I use it on my phone, and it provides 15 feet of calm and peaceful energy.

Explanation of the FLFE Everywhere Bubble

Benefits

Deeper Meditations & Feelings of Calm

Enhanced Creativity

Reduced Anxiety

Immune Support

EMF Mitigation

Improved Sleep

Better Communication

Increased Mental Endurance

Antioxidant Support

GI Tract Support

Decreased Brain Fog

Harmonized Relationships

Energized Nutrients

Grounding Support

Reduction of Stress

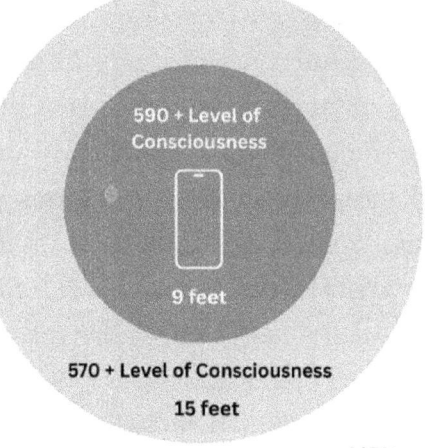

550 Level of Consciousness up to 300 feet

590 + Level of Consciousness
9 feet

570 + Level of Consciousness
15 feet

MPH

10. PETS

I saved the best for last. Some people may not consider a pet a spiritual tool, but God sent them to teach us unconditional love and valuable life lessons. If your childhood left you hurting, the universe may send you a pet who mirrors your heart.

You'll see this pet hesitate in ways you once did—shy, unsure, or too afraid to trust. You'll recognize that flicker of hope when they finally lean into your touch, just like you once wished someone would hold space for you. By loving them through what once broke you, you'll also start to heal that younger version of yourself.

Take it from me, they can heal your heart, soul, and inner child, as you replace hurt with love.

Many people have therapy dogs tailored to their specific needs, whether mentally or physically. Spiritually, they connect on a different level as they are each other's breath, arms, legs, eyes, or voice.

After my traumatic miscarriages and the passing of my cat of 21 years, I felt lost. It wasn't until we got our two pups that I began to heal from being childless not by choice.

My pets mirrored my childhood to the extent that Hans was the blond and beautiful child everyone adored, the Golden Child, representing my older brother in my dysfunctional family. Hannah represented me, the black sheep. She's a petite Yorkie mix full of spunk! Moving fast, even if she trips or hurts herself, she gets back up without hesitation. She's smart, doesn't fall for tricks, and loves with all her heart.

My own mother told me that she cried for three days in the hospital after I was born because I was so ugly! Unlike my plump older brother, with his blond hair and blue eyes, I was tiny and skinny, and constantly crying. When my mom told me this, I was waiting for her to say, 'but you went from an ugly duckling to a beautiful swan,' but she insisted.

At 23, when I announced my pregnancy, she responded, "I'm too young to be a grandma! I don't want to be a grandma!" Then she went into how ugly I was as a baby. At that moment, I knew there was something very wrong with her, but nobody else heard her, and nobody would believe me if I told them what she said. She had complete control over me.

Even though Hannah was the runt, she was a cute puppy with a tiny body and a big personality.

She blossomed into a beautiful young lady with various fur colors: light brown, gray, and blonde. At one time, we had the same hair color, and we continue to share an intense spiritual bond. Hans is a gentle soul, easy-going, and a perfect big brother to Hannah.

Another reason pets make great spiritual tools is their spirit radar. They alert you if any spirits are present in your home. I can tell when visitors arrive because my pet's eyes get huge, then they become timid and try to shrink themselves, as if they're in the presence of God.

When any of these signs occur, I ask them if they encountered this spirit before, and it's usually a yes. Then I ask which ancestor graced us with their presence, and I receive yes or no responses from my pet through my pendulum.

Where there's a will, there's a way. As you can see, it can be a great deal of fun!

Now that you know ten spiritual tools to enhance your healing process, the next chapter will delve into four different ways to help you reach your goals through charts and numbers.

CHAPTER 6

NUMEROLOGY, ASTROLOGY, GENOGRAM, AND CHAKRA CHARTS

Life can be so confusing. It seems like all these things are happening at random, and it's hard to see how you fit into the picture. If only you had a map to guide you.

What if I told you such a map exists? And that this map will become clearer the more you get to know yourself?

Discovering what makes you tick or sets you off makes it easier to reach your goals. You'll be able to avoid wasting time with goals that don't align with your soul's purpose.

When you go for a drive in a new car, don't you want to know what it's good at and not good at, to optimize your experience, and choose a suitable road to get to where you're going? You're not going to drive through a jungle with a golf cart, after all.

This chapter will help you identify your characteristics and discover the person you desire to become. You'll also know which path leading to your goals will be right for you.

NUMEROLOGY

Numerology is one way to uncover your life path. It's fascinating that your date of birth can describe some of your main characteristics and passions.

For example, Life Path Number 5 rang true for me. You see, I dislike repetition. I dislike going to work every day at the same time and same place, doing the same tasks, seeing the same people, and never meeting anyone outside of the office. This is why I chose to be a travel agent, as I crave adventure. Later, I also became a social worker, which allowed me to meet new families through home visits, visit hospitals, attend court hearings, and even visit jails to help my clients.

Numerology helps you:

A. Define your passions
B. Uncover your true personality (which is especially helpful when you feel you've forgotten who you are)
C. Realize your strengths and weaknesses
D. Understand how you interact with others and how others perceive you

What will you discover about yourself?

Your number can be determined using a specific formula and your birthdate. Each number has a different meaning.

August 29, 1966
$8 + 2 + 9 + 1 + 9 + 6 + 6 = 41$
$4 + 1 = 5$

The life path number is therefore five.

Keep in mind, numerology applies to humans, not pets.

So what does each number mean? In the next few pages, you'll find a detailed description of each number.

What Does Your Life Path Number Mean?

1 — High Achiever; Leadership Skills

2 — Compassionate; Mindful & Nurturing

3 — Creative & Self-Expressive

4 — Dedicated; Values Hard Work

5 — Adventurous & Adaptable

6 — Caretaker; Deeply Empathic

7 — Luckiest; Learns New Skills Easily

8 — Savvy & Ambitious; A Leader

9 — Compassionate & Supportive

MPH

LIFE PATH NUMBER 1: THE LEADER

A Life Path Number 1 is a born leader who will follow their dreams and do whatever it takes to become successful. They need to tap into their personal power, leadership skills, and use their motivation to be the very best in whatever they do. Used to success, they secretly fear failure, which keeps them acting fast and changing their plans to win.

What describes a Life Path Number 1:

- Confident
- Motivated
- Determined to reach their dreams
- Hard worker
- Leader
- Driven
- Independent
- Flexible

Good at: Manifesting, reaching whatever goal they set, being flexible

Struggle with: not coming across as arrogant, getting other people to cooperate and uphold the same work ethics, not being critical of self or others

LIFE PATH NUMBER 2: THE PEACEMAKER

A Life Path Number 2 thrives when helping others, especially in group projects, and their goal is to establish harmony within any relationship. They value relationships with family, romantic partners, friends, and colleagues on a long-term basis. These chronic people-pleasers never put their needs first, which can lead to resentment. To avoid being hurt, they'll withdraw.

What describes a Life Path Number 2:

- Generous
- Peacemaker
- Harmonious
- Sensitive
- Detail-oriented
- Intuitive
- Compassionate

Good at: being unbiased, using their intuition and big heart to create harmony in the world

Struggle with: putting their needs first, confrontations, not taking everything personally

LIFE PATH NUMBER 3: THE CREATIVE

A Life Path Number 3 believes everything will work out. They live in the moment, embrace life with a high vibration, and are great communicators. These people-oriented individuals thrive through self-expression, communication, and having fun. They value having brilliant ideas and an active social life.

What describes a Life Path Number 3:

- Communicator
- Social butterfly
- Magnetic
- Outspoken
- Positive
- Creative
- Optimistic
- Fun

Good at: finding the positive in any situation, rallying people for a cause, expressing themselves, making friends

Struggle with: commitment, forming deep emotional bonds, handling money and responsibilities

LIFE PATH NUMBER 4: THE MANAGER

A Life Path Number 4 is great at putting the pieces together, works hard, and makes a great teacher. Ensuring security and stability is their game plan. They thrive when they have a plan, remain organized, and are committed. What matters to them is honesty, trust, fidelity in relationships, and an organized house.

What describes a Life Path Number 4:

- Hard worker
- Grounded
- Down to earth
- Patient
- Dependable
- Practical
- Disciplined
- Stable
- Loyal

Good at: teaching others due to their confidence and knowledge, being logical, putting the pieces together, sticking to the plan

Struggle with: being too judgmental of themselves and others, thinking outside of the box, accepting change, taking advantage of opportunities

LIFE PATH NUMBER 5: THE ADVENTURER

A Life Path Number 5 would make a great traveling salesman. Routine is unbearable, and they want to experience all that life has to offer. These explorers thrive on change, freedom, meeting new people, and daily new experiences. They value living in the moment, being their own boss, and trying new things. However, relationships can become complicated due to fickleness and a strong need for change. Ultimately, they fear being trapped in a relationship.

What describes a Life Path Number 5:

- Adventurous
- Experimental
- Freedom
- Loves learning
- Travel enthusiast
- People-lover

Good at: interacting with people, being flexible and ready for anything

Struggle with: commitment, routine, finding a life purpose

LIFE PATH NUMBER 6: THE NURTURER

A Life Path Number 6 aims to be responsible, fair, and of service to others. Wanting to please others, they become the nurturer within their group. They thrive by leading with their heart while serving loved ones and being a caretaker (and sometimes serving justice as well).

What describes a Life Path Number 6:

- Nurturing
- Loving
- Protective

- Compassionate
- Respectful
- Understanding
- Kind
- Controlling

Good at: being a parent, nurturing their families, friends, and communities

Struggle with: giving too much to others, not taking care of their own needs, not becoming an enabler

LIFE PATH NUMBER 7: THE SEEKER

Through their spirituality, a Life Path Number 7 searches for the meaning of life. These philosophers thrive when uncovering the secrets of life and the universe, problem-solving, and spending time in nature (alone). They value their alone time, nature, knowledge, and spirituality. Their solitude can make it hard for them to find close relationships.

What describes a Life Path Number 7:

- Inner wisdom
- Curious
- Spiritual
- Thorough
- Truthful
- Intuitive
- Nature lover
- Knowledgeable

Good at: diving deeper for a solution, uncovering the truth, being analytical

Struggle with: having faith, romantic relationships, not overanalyzing

LIFE PATH NUMBER 8: THE POWERHOUSE

A Life Path Number 8 focuses on achievements, financial wealth, status, and ambition. These business executives thrive when they feel accomplished and enjoy the financial rewards that show their efforts. They value their status, material wealth, reputation, and ability to provide for their family. However, because they don't feel safe unless they have a substantial amount of money, they can become workaholics and neglect their relationships.

What describes a Life Path Number 8:

- Hard worker
- Materialistic
- Realistic
- Leader
- Successful
- Ambitious
- Workaholic
- Authoritative
- Controlling

Good at: leading others, working hard, crushing goals

Struggle with: relaxation, feeling safe and secure (it's never enough), accepting what they can't control

LIFE PATH NUMBER 9: THE HUMANITARIAN

A Life Path Number 9 is a huge giver, almost to a fault, and spiritual. These humanitarians thrive when they are helping others and making the world a better place. An obstacle is an opportunity to learn. They value their life experiences, which brought them self-awareness and inner strength. Their generosity may cause financial problems.

What describes a Life Path Number 9:

- Humanitarian
- Spiritual
- Intuitive
- Religious
- Compassionate
- Integrity
- Acceptance
- Generous

Good at: taking care of others, providing support, giving advice

Struggle with: letting go of the past, putting their needs first, conflict, facing negative emotions

ASTROLOGY

Astrology is another way to help you understand yourself better. To me, it represents a form of self-love because knowledge is power. There are 12 zodiac signs, assigned based on your birth date. Each sign receives a message each day, called a daily horoscope.

Aries (March 21 – April 19)
Taurus (April 20 - May 20)
Gemini (May 21 - June 21)
Cancer (June 22 - July 22)
Leo (July 23 - August 22)
Virgo (August 23 - September 22)
Libra (September 23 - October 23)

Scorpio (October 24 - November 21)
Sagittarius (November 22 - December 21)
Capricorn (December 22 - January 19)
Aquarius (January 20 - February 18)
Pisces (February 19 - March 20)

Then each sign is sorted into four categories: Fire, Earth, Air, and Water.

Fire Signs (Aries, Leo, Sagittarius) – are considered passionate and expressive.

Earth Signs (Taurus, Virgo, Capricorn) – are considered practical and grounded.

Air Signs (Gemini, Libra, Aquarius) – are considered intelligent and curious.

Water Signs (Cancer, Scorpio, Pisces) – are considered intuitive and emotional.

Sometimes, you'll find that your astrological sign doesn't seem to describe you fully. This discrepancy is because most people only consider the sun sign.

With a complete astrological chart (basically a snapshot of how the planets were aligned when you were born), a sign is assigned to each planet, and each planet corresponds to a different facet of your personality. For example, the moon represents your underlying emotions, Venus describes how you love and experience relationships, and Mercury represents your communication style.

For now, let's go over three of the most important ones: your rising sign, sun sign, and moon sign.

What is a rising sign? This sign corresponds to the time you were born and is considered the "mask" you wear when interacting with others; this is how others see you.

What is a sun sign? This sign corresponds with the actual day of your birth and determines your identity, personality, and core.

What is a moon sign? This sign comes from the moon's position at the time of your birth and signifies your emotions and feelings.

There are resources available online to calculate your rising and moon sign.

The above definitions helped me understand why I have what I call a split personality. I'm a Virgo with a Leo rising sign, and Leo embodies characteristics that are the opposite of Virgo. This combination explains why I sometimes prefer to stay behind the scenes, even though I'm also comfortable in the limelight. My moon sign is Aquarius, reflecting my need for fairness, my free spirit, and how I thrive on independence and solving problems uniquely.

Let me explain what an astrological chart is and how it can help you on your journey. As I mentioned, it provides a snapshot of how the moon and stars aligned at the time of your birth.

An astrologer can give you insight into what to expect moving forward and explain how the planets may affect your chemistry, as each day holds new meaning based on the location of the stars and planets. That's why people who've been waiting on a wish always say, I have to wait until the moon and stars align before I can (_insert task_).

Additionally, your chart is divided into 12 houses, each covering a different aspect of your life. To obtain a full reading, an astrologer uses your date of birth, the time you were born, and the city where you were born. They then locate your first house, moving counter-clockwise from there.

12 Houses of Astrology

1st House
Personality
Ego
Self-Image
Beginnings
Consciousness
Appearance
Temperament

2nd House
Material
Possessions
Finances
Assets
Physical Body
Earnings
Financial Loans

3rd House
Perception
Curiosity
Communication
Early Education
Technology
Siblings
Extended Family

4th House
Ancestry
Home
Family
Roots
Youth
Mother
Genetics

5th House
Passion
Fun
Self-Expression
Pleasure
Inner Child
Children
Casual Sex

6th House
Health
Wellness
Duty
Service
Work
Healing
Pets Daily Routines

7th House
Relationships
Partnerships
Marriage
Life Partners
Business Partners
Relating
Foreign Affairs

8th House
Transformation
Sex
Death
Taboos
Magic
Inheritance
Other Outside Money

9th House
Travel
Spirituality
Seeking
Philosophy
Expansion
Legal
Higher Education

10th House
Career
Ambition
Reputation
Power
Dominant Parent
Fame
Social Status

11th House
Wishes
Social Circle
Earned Wealth
Community
Collective
Friendship
Philanthropy

12th House
Dreams
Fears
Fantasies
Addiction
Secrets
Hidden Desires
Unconsciousness

MPH

Your astrology birth chart serves as a window into your soul's journey, as everything aligns as it should.

Birth charts provide valuable insights into your potential strengths and weaknesses, when to hold major life events (such as marriage or moving into a new home), what type of career suits you, and why you're attracted to certain people and not others.

GENOGRAM

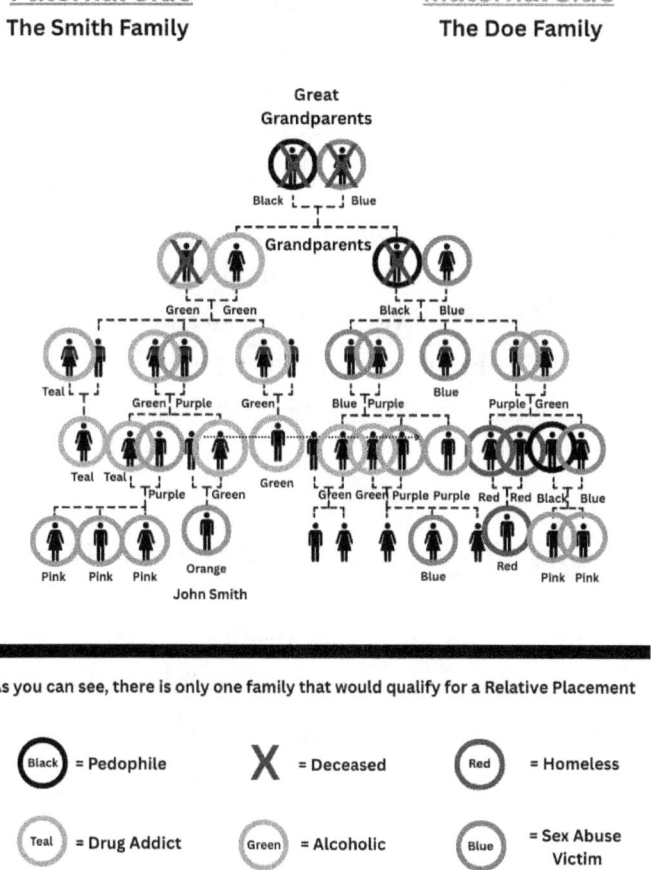

A genogram is a tool used by social workers and other professionals to determine family patterns related to abuse or neglect. At Children's Services, I had to complete one for each family on my caseload to prepare in case the child needed a family placement.

Once all the information is collected, it will indicate who has a criminal record, who suffers from alcoholism or mental health issues, who is divorced, who has died, and who is blood-related to the child.

This chart served at the family's Mediation Meetings, when determining the abused child's new home.

One time, I needed to write one on a chalkboard for a mom who was in jail and had multiple fathers for her eight children. It revealed the dysfunctional family dynamics across three generations, and made it evident that the grandmother would be the only qualified primary caregiver for all eight children. This case was tough, but also one of my success stories. I helped the grandmother obtain custody of her grandchildren while Mom was frequently in and out of jail.

This chart has valuable information for the family and serves as a motivator to stop the cycles of generational abuse.

CHAKRA CHARTS FOR HUMANS AND PETS

For those of you who want a quick overview of the chakras and what they're associated with, several charts are available online as a reference guide. These charts contain information related to your emotions, physical health, and ways to incorporate healing practices with your chakras.

Some diagrams illustrate which crystals to use, others associate angels, or provide detailed information about your emotions and actions.

This image is an example of a basic chart:

CHAPTER 6: NUMEROLOGY, ASTROLOGY, GENOGRAM, AND CHAKRA CHARTS | **105**

The Seven Chakras

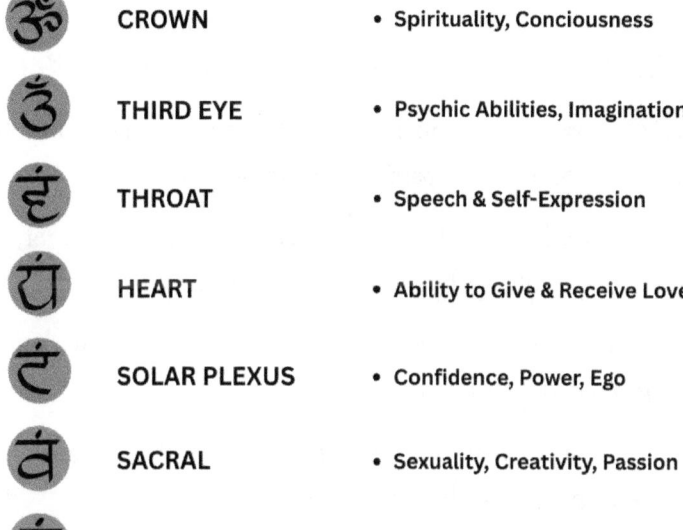

MPH

I use a chart for pets to determine which behavior is associated with which chakra. This association wasn't something I learned in class. I discovered it while doing research and tested these theories for many years. It's amazing how similar pets are to humans.

When your chakras are out of balance, they trigger issues that can derail your life. This overview is for humans, but below is a list of which chakra triggers which negative behaviors.

Negative Behaviors Triggered By Chakras:

1. Root Chakra – fear, instability, anxiety, ungroundedness, poor boundaries, materialism, laziness, hoarding, overeating.
2. Sacral Chakra – emotional instability, poor social skills, fear of change, lack of desire or passion, sex addiction.
3. Solar Plexus Chakra – Low self-esteem, self-doubt, anger, victim mentality, controlling, hyperactive, power hungry.
4. Heart Chakra – lack of trust, fear of rejection, antisocial, depression, narcissism, co-dependency, jealousy.
5. Throat Chakra – fear of speaking, intrusive thoughts, shy, weak voice, talking incessantly, gossiping, interrupting
6. Third Eye Chakra – unable to make decisions, poor memory, insensitive, frequent nightmares, obsessive
7. Crown Chakra – lack of purpose or feeling disconnected, not spiritual, difficulty learning, confusion

My hope is for you to use these tools to get to know yourself better. To find a balance between your strengths and weaknesses, and how to become your best selves. To understand how the public perceives you, how your characteristics influence your life, and how to overcome challenges.

Also, these tools help you understand your relationships, career, goals, challenges, and accomplishments.

The next chapter will help you evaluate your progress. It will show you where you are on your healing journey, what changes you may need to make, and what strengths to focus on going forward.

CHAPTER 7

HOW DO I KNOW IF I'M HEALED?

You may ask yourself, "How do I know if I'm healed?" Healing from trauma is a long journey, and only you can answer this question. Remember that a full recovery can take a while, but you'll continue to get better. Always celebrate improvements and take it one step at a time.

In this chapter, take a quick quiz to see how far along the path of healing you are, and then I'll answer the same questions in detail from my life experiences for added context. Keep in mind that all human beings suffer from some sort of trauma, even the people you view as 'the happiest you know' won't get a perfect score.

Be honest with yourself: there is no right or wrong, only how far you've come. Go easy on yourself and keep moving forward.

QUIZ: HOW MUCH HAVE I HEALED?

1. Do you feel the need to explain yourself?

    A. Always, they might judge/ misunderstand
    B. Often, yes, to avoid trouble
    C. Sometimes, it depends on the situation/person
    D. Not anymore, I don't care what anyone thinks

2. Do you allow yourself to feel emotions?

    A. No
    B. Rarely
    C. Often
    D. All the time

3. Do you react less to stressors?

    A. No, I still get very upset
    B. Sometimes I'm able to put it behind me
    C. Most of the time
    D. It doesn't affect me anymore

4. Do you release tension or trauma through exercise regularly?

    A. No. I don't exercise
    B. I sometimes exercise twice a week
    C. I often exercise twice a week
    D. I always exercise at least twice a week

5. Have you stopped walking on eggshells?

    A. No, I still do
    B. Sometimes
    C. Most of the time
    D. Yes! I speak and act freely

6. Do you experience unconditional love in your relationships?

   A. Not really, I wish
   B. Rarely
   C. Sometimes
   D. Yes

7. Can you tell your story without strong emotions?

   A. No, it feels like it happened yesterday
   B. Occasionally, I manage to hold it in
   C. More and more, except when I'm feeling low
   D. Yes, I'm over it now

8. Do you practice self-love?

   A. No, I don't even know what that is
   B. Rarely
   C. Sometimes
   D. Yes, regularly

9. Have you learned to accept a compliment?

   A. I'm really bad at accepting compliments
   B. I accept the rare compliment
   C. I accept compliments now, for the most part
   D. I accept compliments with ease and grace

10. Do you feel physically safe?

    A. No, not all
    B. Rarely
    C. Sometimes
    D. Yes, all the time

11. Do you have healthy boundaries?

    A. I don't know how to set boundaries
    B. My boundaries are like a straw house
    C. My boundaries are like a wooden fence
    D. My boundaries are reinforced brick walls

12. Do you experience intense memories or flashbacks?

    A. Yes, all the time, it's like I'm living it all over again
    B. Quite often
    C. Sometimes, but much less than before
    D. Not anymore

13. Do you sleep like a dinosaur? *(T-Rex position, with your hands tucked in to your chest)*

    A. All the time, I find it comforting
    B. Sometimes
    C. Rarely
    D. Never

14. Are you codependent or a people pleaser?

    A. Yes, I don't want others to hate/leave me
    B. For the most part, I rarely do what I want
    C. Less than before, I do more things for myself now
    D. Not anymore, I live my own life

15. Are you a workaholic or always on the go?

    A. Yes, sitting still makes me restless/ feel guilty
    B. Usually, I struggle to relax/ find time
    C. Less than before
    D. Not anymore, I prioritize relaxation and "me" time

16. Are you a perfectionist?

   A. Yes, I can't help it
   B. More often than not
   C. I'm a recovering perfectionist
   D. I'm now able to let go and accept things as they are

17. Can you confidently make decisions?

   A. I doubt every decision and struggle to commit
   B. A decision rarely comes easily
   C. I doubt some decisions, but it's getting better
   D. I easily decide, knowing it will work out somehow

18. Have you made peace with [insert your trauma] and developed coping mechanisms for your triggers?

   A. No, it still paralyzes me
   B. There has been some progress, but it's a real struggle
   C. I slip up from time to time, but I'm doing a lot better
   D. Yes, even when it resurfaces in new ways, I can handle it

19. Do you trust yourself to make decisions concerning your future?

   A. No, I'll just mess everything up
   B. Rarely, I'm not good at making decisions like that
   C. Sometimes I do, and sometimes I don't
   D. Yes, I will make the decision that's right for me

20. Do you feel better emotionally and physically?

   A. No, I still feel miserable
   B. Sometimes
   C. More often than not
   D. Yes, I feel like I released the weight I kept carrying

Scoring: Keep in mind that this number will change continuously throughout your journey. Add up your letters and calculate your total amount of points to find out which stage you're in right now.

- A - 0 points
- B - 1 point
- C - 2 points
- D - 3 points

0 - 8 points – You're in the bud stage.

Congratulations. The first step is the hardest, but you did it! A mirror can be intimidating because it shows you what is and not what you'd like to see. It takes a brave soul to look at herself honestly and take action to change. Keep up the momentum. Many small steps will add up to a big difference in the end.

9 - 22 points – You're in the half-bloom stage.

Layer by layer, you create the foundation for your new way of life. You may trip and slide into old habits, but you're determined to change and are starting to catch yourself. Maybe you feel vulnerable, as if you're exposing yourself to the world, but the world needs to see the real you. Keep going!

23 - 36 points – You're in the bloom stage.

Look at you go! You have made significant progress and are well on your way to recovery. When your thoughts get dark, it might be tempting to withdraw, but you don't let it stop you. Sure, you may slip up now and then (part of being human), but you catch yourself much faster than before.

37 - 50 points – You're in the fruit-bearing stage.

You're getting the hang of it. You worked hard and have come a long way from when you first decided to overcome this trauma. It may seem like it's good enough now, but don't let up yet. Continue catching all the sneaky ways this trauma tries to mess with what you do and who you are (it will make the difference between trimming the weeds back and uprooting them entirely).

51 - 60 points – You're in the seed dispersal stage.

Reward yourself for coming this far. We often focus on moving from task to task, but rehabilitation is hard work. While freedom from your trauma in and of itself is sweeter than any birthday cake (at this point, it's a re-birthday cake), think of something symbolic (and lasting, or both if you want cake) you can give yourself. Choose a visual reminder of the progress you made and that you can overcome any other trauma knocking on your door.

You're so much stronger than you think, and as a living example of what's possible, you can help others overcome their trauma too.

QUESTION OVERVIEW

Over the next few pages, I answered and illustrated each question to help you clarify where you are on the spectrum of healing and what's possible for you.

If you found a particular question challenging to answer, or simply wish to know more, you'll find everything you need here.

Let's get started.

1. Do you feel the need to explain yourself?

Being misunderstood can be an enormous source of frustration. People often assume the worst and are unwilling to hear the truth afterward. To avoid someone getting angry for no reason or you losing something you hold dear, you explain desperately. It becomes a reflex, a source of protection from anticipated painful consequences.

Always the scapegoat as a child, no one believed me if I said I didn't do it. It had to be my fault, and I couldn't defend myself.

As an adult, I became louder and tried to stand up for myself. Maybe I'm misunderstood because I'm an INFJ, the oddest personality combination in the world, with only three percent of the population displaying these traits.

Being perceived as odd can cause you to become an outcast within your community, without a clear cause.

An example of this was when I attended high school in Anderson Township, where two Maureens of the same age attended different high schools. The other Maureen had a reputation as a bad girl.

People thought I was her, even though I didn't know she existed.

My reputation plummeted as I shouldered the societal responsibilities for things I never did. No one bothered to find out more about her or me. They just assumed that I was 'that kind of person'.

It wasn't until many years later that I finally reached the point where I no longer cared what people thought. It surprised me, to be honest. Constantly defending myself as a child and young adult wore me out until I realized it didn't matter. I knew who I was. My actions spoke louder than words, and I never intentionally tried to hurt someone.

From that point on, I didn't feel the need to explain myself to anyone anymore. Instead of wasting valuable time and energy anticipating people's reactions, I just did what I wanted.

What about you?

When you think, "I don't care what they think of me," and follow your desires freely, you know you've healed. Let other people think whatever they want. Their judgments are a reflection of their own fears and societal conditioning; it has nothing to do with you.

2. Do you allow yourself to feel emotions?

When experiencing trauma, you tend to push your feelings away, hoping you'll forget, or numb them with alcohol or drugs. This reaction is common, and you might tell yourself that you're self-medicating, but the side effects can be overwhelming and ineffective.

Feeling your emotions is part of the healing process.

Crying, shouting, or hitting your pillow can be beneficial. It allows you to release stuck emotions, making it easier to process the reasons behind them before letting go.

I grew up numb. Once I left for college, I had no idea who I even was, because it never felt safe to be myself. This feeling only changed once medications corrected my brain chemistry, and I took the time to feel, understand, and release my emotions.

3. Do you react less to stressors?

Have you stopped laughing off or downplaying traumatic events? I have, but it took a while. Laughter is beneficial during tough times. However, you minimize your situation to sidestep the pain.

Your triggers guide you toward healing. Once you pinpoint why this became a sensitive situation, you understand where the feelings originated and find out how to counteract defensive mechanisms instead of allowing the triggers to control you.

A good example was when I attended my brother's wedding.

At that time, my parents had already disowned me, for reasons I'll never know. When I was 26, my mom called me. "You have too many problems, and we, your dad and I, are cutting ties. You're no longer a part of the family."

They were my only family in California. There were no aunts, uncles, cousins, or grandparents. I started to hyperventilate and tremble after the call, so you can imagine the courage it took for me to show up to the wedding.

Refusing to miss my brother's wedding, I found a solution without laughing off my pain. I took control of the situation and prepared my words. With my sister and her husband backing me up, I walked into the reception. After a quick "Hello, you look nice," to my mom, I kept walking.

That's called killing your enemy with kindness. She brightened up, smiled, and soaked that compliment into her narcissistic brain. When you can make 'nice' in public and not make a scene, you're on your way to healing.

4. Do you release tension or trauma through exercise regularly?

Do you allow yourself to release through tears and truly feel the pain? Sometimes tears flow without you realizing you're crying. It's a good way to assess the intensity of a situation.

As a child, I never got to cry because I always needed to stay quiet. I've found it's a quick way to release tension in my body while experiencing intense emotions.

Another way to release bottled-up emotions is through exercise.

Have you tried yoga or physical exercise, such as swimming, to eliminate stuck energy? It's crucial to release these emotions before they develop into disease.

Exercise became my preferred form of meditation ever since I was old enough to join a gym. Before that, I'd take walks, ride a bike, or swim. Luckily, I released stored trauma as I was growing up, and I didn't even know it since I was already an active child.

5. Have you stopped walking on eggshells?

This defense mechanism is a big issue that gets little attention, as we prefer to let sleeping dragons lie. You adjust to your abuser's mood and avoid confronting them about their actions. You know what will happen if you do. It will be your fault, and any important event will be canceled.

Holding your tongue and restricting your movements so you don't set them off becomes the norm.

I walked on eggshells until I was 29, after my divorce. Growing up, my mom would often cancel our holidays at the last minute, so everyone followed orders and walked on tiptoes to maintain the peace.

My cousin called me 'ninja' because I could leave a room at night without making a sound. I learned this skill while sharing a Jack-n-Jill bathroom with my parents as a child. It got so bad that I wouldn't flush the toilet for fear of waking my mom.

My behavior persisted when I got married, and I did everything possible to avoid confrontation. Finally, I couldn't ignore it anymore, and I asked for a separation that turned into a divorce once I left the house.

Let me tell you, it felt like a huge weight fell off my shoulders. I was now responsible only for myself, and I enjoyed my newfound freedom.

6. Do you experience unconditional love in your relationships?

Unconditional love is something all human beings deserve and desire, yet often we settle for less out of desperation.

As the scapegoat, I needed to earn my mother's love, although I didn't realize it would never come. She was unable to love anyone, not even herself, due to her childhood trauma.

Have you discovered what a healthy relationship is and how to navigate your differences and choices?

It took me a long time to understand what a narcissist was, and I suffered for a long time because I didn't know any better. Once I figured it out, I found wonderful friends who would go to the ends of the earth for me, unlike my parents.

Eventually, I met someone to marry who treated me like a princess and allowed me to be myself. I never knew unconditional love until I was 38, but it was worth the wait.

7. Can you tell your story without strong emotions?

Sometimes when you tell a story, emotions flare up as if it happened recently, even if it took place years or even decades ago. Even if you calm down after a while, every time you remember what happened, feelings surge once more.

A lady once interrupted me while I shared my story and asked me, "How can you talk about losing a child without crying?"

Why? Because I healed from the trauma and released it, as it happened 10 years ago. I have a lot to look forward to when I go to heaven because I get to meet my three babies: Hans, Hannah, and Maria.

It doesn't mean that it no longer holds any meaning; you simply choose to acknowledge it without letting it control you and prevent you from enjoying the present. It's an event that took place, and it'll always be a part of you, but it no longer defines you or your choices.

Once you can detach the past from the present, you're ready to help others with their pain.

8. Do you practice self-love?

Self-love can be difficult because if the people who were supposed to love you unconditionally didn't, then who would?

For many years, that was my mentality, until I began to learn about angels. These beings see us as beautifully unique and bright lights of love, so I started to do the same.

People who don't love themselves make choices that are far from in their best interest.

That's why I took a year off after my divorce and permitted myself not to make any significant decisions to give myself time to heal. That's when my spiritual awakening occurred, and I practiced daily self-love by breathing in love and releasing fear. No one taught me this method, but it seemed right at the time.

I started to prioritize myself because you can't save anyone from drowning while drowning yourself.

9. Have you learned to accept a compliment?

Accepting a compliment is harder than it may seem. Perhaps you feel unworthy of such praise because you struggle to love yourself, or having to live up to the pedestal someone just put you on frightens you.

At 21, while working as a travel agent, I set a goal to learn how to accept compliments graciously.

I never received a compliment from my parents, and to this day, I still haven't. When men stared or whistled at me, I'd get angry and wonder why they looked my way.

It took me many years to realize and accept that I was beautiful.

Once you learn to love yourself and see yourself for the talented and amazing being you are, you'll be able to accept compliments without doubting their sincerity.

10. Do you feel physically safe?

When you experience a traumatic event, you lack control over the situation, and this terrifies you. This fear invades your daily life, keeping you stuck and preventing you from moving forward. It influences every choice you make.

I always felt safe when I lived alone because I knew my angels divinely protected me.

After separating from my husband and moving into my friend's apartment, I began to notice something strange. There were clicking noises coming from my closet sliding door. When I asked about it, she said, "Oh, those are the angels, I hear those too." I wondered why an angel would be hanging out in my bedroom.

This conversation was the first time I heard about angels being real, and I soon realized they weren't just in my bedroom, but accompanied me wherever I went.

11. Do you have healthy boundaries?

People starving for love often overextend themselves into someone's life or isolate themselves, neither of which is good.

For example, if you suffered from sexual abuse, did you feel stripped of your innocence, making you feel years wiser than you should have been at a young age? Have you found appropriate boundaries concerning someone touching you, or if you're still in a domestic violence situation, do you have an escape route?

These boundaries can be as simple as becoming a 'non-hugger' in a world of touchy-feely people.

I grew up without hugs or gentle touches. It wasn't normal for me to reciprocate a hug, no matter how well-intentioned. To protect my space, I let others know that 'I wasn't a hugger' until I felt safe enough to embrace others.

12. Do you experience intense memories or flashbacks?

Traumatic flashbacks can be debilitating. No matter how strong your desire to move on with your life, you can completely freeze up.

It's challenging to control flashbacks, but I was able to overcome mine through an energy technique called Amygdala Trauma Release. It helps you step out of fight-or-flight mode, regulate your emotions, and release trapped trauma.

This Healing Touch for Animals® technique from Chapter 4 can also be applied to humans.

While providing a distance session, I used myself as the surrogate, allowing myself to receive at the same time as the client. This treatment completely stopped my PTSD flashbacks, and worked wonders on other clients I provided this technique to as well.

13. Do you sleep like a dinosaur?

T-rex arms is a term used when you tuck your hands in and bend your wrists close to your chest to feel safe. I was surprised to learn that this was a trauma response, although it makes perfect sense. It's a position that offers both protection and comfort.

As a child, I always slept on my side, hugging my pillow with my hands tucked in next to my chest.

Even though I worked through my issues, I'll continue to sleep like a dinosaur because of the comfort it brings. What matters in this case is that it's a conscious choice, and not a need.

14. Are you codependent or a people-pleaser?

You might fear being hated, or worse, abandoned. Perhaps people will think less of you for refusing. They might call you selfish or inconsiderate. All these things and more go through your head when you need to make a decision.

When asked for a favor, I couldn't say no. This behavior continued until I was in my 30s. I remember the exact moment I first said no. It didn't go over very well, but that wasn't my problem.

Prioritize your own needs and secure your oxygen mask before helping anyone. It's easy to take advantage of nice people, so limit the amount of time and attention you give.

Co-dependent relationships are tricky, especially if you're married, but maintaining independence within a marriage is essential. Being independent doesn't mean you don't care about your partner; instead, it means you take time to go out with the girls, and skip going to the store with your spouse or joining the guys' trip.

Healing from co-dependency involves establishing healthy boundaries within a relationship.

15. Are you a workaholic or always on the go?

This trauma response signals you're still in fight-or-flight mode. Avoiding your problems, behaviors, or thoughts by staying busy doesn't give you the time to process your emotions.

Many people try to go back to their routine right after the death of a family member. The emotions bubbling up when they stop to think become overwhelming. It seems easier to keep moving, although it will eventually catch up to them.

These workaholics aren't living, they're surviving. It's just like an addiction:

A workaholic only feels good when they're working.

An alcoholic only feels good when they're drinking.

Running away from your emotions merely keeps you stuck on a hamster wheel, unable to move forward. As Whitney Houston once sang, 'You can't run from yourself, there's nowhere to hide'.

16. Are you a perfectionist?

Many people don't realize that perfectionism is a trauma response. It leads to extreme anxiety and feelings of being overwhelmed. No one can be perfect. You set yourself up for failure if you try. There's nothing wrong with giving it your best shot.

You're perfect in God's and your Guardian Angel's eyes.

That said, I'm guilty of this. Virgos, like myself, are born perfectionists, and it can be hard to let go. Others lived with parents who made them feel they needed to be the best in everything, and that's not possible.

What you need to realize is that perfectionism is a mask. What are you trying to cover up? What don't you want people to see?

17. Can you confidently make decisions?

Part of trauma recovery is rediscovering yourself without outside influences. If you can't make decisions, it may be a sign of depression or feeling overwhelmed and stuck.

When I feel stuck, I get up and walk, run, bike, or simply move. Physical motion gets your energy moving, releases endorphins, and takes your mind off your problems. Another idea is to inhale essential oils to stimulate your mind. Afterwards, I'm more productive and can make decisions more easily.

However, if you're in the early stages of recovery, you may be in shock, and your body has shut down to protect you. When you feel more like yourself, you're on the way to recovery.

18. Have you made peace with [insert your trauma] and developed coping mechanisms for your triggers?

My trauma is being childless. I desperately wanted a child, but struggled to get pregnant and miscarried multiple times. In our current society, fertility issues happen more and more often.

There are numerous triggers for this part of the population as everyone around them starts to have children, and they're still on the sidelines, waiting. Then, when they think they're fine, along come the grandchildren they don't have, and their heart breaks again. Every holiday becomes a trigger due to the absence of children at their celebrations.

My suggestion is to start your own family traditions for the holidays, even if it's just yourself.

Setting boundaries is the only way to protect yourself from triggers, although it's hard because children and pregnant women are everywhere.

One boundary in particular meant disconnecting with a good friend who got pregnant while I miscarried three times. I had to pull out of her life. It was for emotional safety, as I hadn't healed enough to support her, and she's still mad to this day.

You have to know your limits.

19. Do you trust yourself to make decisions concerning your future?

Survivors of narcissist abuse doubt their capabilities, memory, ability to communicate, and even their value as a human being. Gaslighting makes you even doubt reality itself.

If this person is still in your life, it's unlikely you'll be able to heal because of the ongoing abuse. Once you step away, your thoughts will be clearer, and you'll soon realize it was never your fault and that you're a very competent person.

Celebrate it!

20. Do you feel better emotionally and physically?

Signs that your body is physically healing include improved sleep, return of appetite, increased energy, and a decrease in symptoms of fatigue or pain. These signs can be subtle, but indicate that the body is restoring balance and recovering.

When I was in survival mode and working full-time, I developed IBS. I knew it was from my unresolved trauma and my second-hand trauma, plus the foods I ate didn't help.

Once I changed jobs, it disappeared. Now, I'm happy to say, I'm the healthiest I've ever been in my life. I feel good, inside and out!

WHAT ABOUT YOU?

How are you feeling about yourself right now? You worked hard. Make sure to celebrate your efforts, no matter how small (this is how to motivate yourself to continue).

Come back to this quiz as often as you need to. As I mentioned before, where you're at now is not where you'll always be. As you continue to work on yourself, your score will get higher, and your trauma will have less power over you.

It's time to free yourself from the weight of the past that has been holding you down.

WHAT IS THE MEANING OF LIFE?

Dear Earth Angel,

I'd like you to think about this question: "What is the meaning of life?"

To me, it's LOVE. Plain and simple. Everybody wants to be loved, but it's not for sale. You can't pick it up at the store. It's a powerful feeling that can swell with overwhelming amounts of joy, or diminish with intense self-hatred.

Self-love is the key remedy to heal any trauma. If you can appreciate yourself for who you have become despite your hardships, treat yourself with kindness, and think positively... you've won! You found the meaning of life.

Once you love yourself, you attract other forms of love. The more love, the better. Don't ever give up the fight. Keep your hope and integrity intact.

I want to end my story on a positive note, after sharing some of the unfortunate ones, so you can see what's possible for you. I've accomplished quite a bit on my own, so don't let anyone tell you it's not possible. My guidance counselor at the University of Cincinnati said it's impossible to work full-time, take two classes, and work 15 hours a week in an unpaid internship for three quarters.

After I graduated, I made sure to visit her office so she could congratulate me on my accomplishment. Boy, did she eat her words. I did this so she wouldn't discourage anyone else in the future. Had I listened to her, I wouldn't be here writing this book.

Since I was living in California against my will at the age of 21, I decided to take advantage of the opportunity to travel. I took a certified course on the travel industry's computer system and became a travel agent. I was in the right place at the right time.

In my first job, I worked at a call center, selling Hawaii packages from California. At 21, with no obligations, I traveled to Hawaii for free on four different occasions.

I will never forget how excited I was for my first trip while packing my carry-on. Running around the room, I threw items into my suitcase. We only found out the day before that the agency had chosen us to leave the next morning. While packing, I couldn't stop eating the Oreo cookies stashed in my room. My intense excitement turned into uncontrollable snacking (which I don't recommend).

Shaking my head, I kept saying to myself, "Me? Little old me from Ohio is going to Hawaii!" It felt like I won the lottery because I was only making $6.50 an hour and had been living with my parents.

Together with my roommate, who was also a friend from work, we explored all the hotels and sights, which we could then sell when we returned to the mainland.

Treated like royalty, we stayed in luxurious hotels, were wined and dined, and transported in limousines, all while being adorned with beautiful leis. Additionally, they supplied us with chocolate-covered macadamia nuts, pineapples, and champagne.

Each time I returned, I visited a different island and even got married at the Kapiʻolani Park in Oahu at sunset.

I flew numerous times within the 50 states, visited Mexico three times, and Jamaica four times. While living in California, every weekend was a road trip. I visited San Francisco, Monterey, Carmel, Santa Cruz, Lake Tahoe, Reno, and drove up and down the coast twice (once with college friends, known as the 'Ohio girls', and once when I was married). Santa Barbara was my favorite, and I loved San Diego so much I almost moved there.

Even though I had a good life after my divorce, people would sadly say, "I'm so sorry about your divorce," because that was the standard saying. I'd respond, "Don't be. I'm not! This was my decision!" It felt like I was paving the way for future divorcees and taking away the shame of it all.

I changed travel agent jobs frequently to increase my salary, even though it was only $1.00 more per hour at a time.

So when I left Castro Travel, the owner asked me why I was leaving, and I said, "Because I didn't get a raise." They tried to lure me back with a raise, but I declined. "No, I'm happy with my decision." Then, unbeknownst to me, before that day ended, the entire department got raises.

One friend was hanging out of a moving car window in the parking lot, chanting 'Norma Rae, Norma Rae' as she pumped her arm, pretending she had muscles.

I worked in the travel industry for 10 years, transitioning to corporate travel, where I served business travelers from prominent companies such as Apple, Sun, Yahoo, and Google.

When I decided to move back to Cincinnati, the agency I worked for needed a 'traveling travel agent'. I was sent to different cities to fill in for vacations, and all expenses were covered. Soon, the managers at the offices would ask me for the 'temperature' of their staff. I was their informant, and it was fun, although I made sure to make general statements.

This company flew me to my first assignment out of state and shipped my furniture and car to Cincinnati, where I relocated. When I returned to Cincinnati after ten years, I was a different person.

By then, I'd learned to be independent and watch out for myself, because if I didn't, who would?

I overcame being a Caucasian who married into a Hispanic family and the stigma of being divorced, which was taboo in 1997. Expanding my worldview, I learned about different cultures, customs, and traditions while living in diversity.

My spiritual awakening started, and soon I needed to find a new career, as the travel benefits disappeared once the public could book tickets online.

Deciding to return to college at UC, I aimed to become a social worker. That took three years, while I worked full-time and supported myself. In my early 30s, I could easily navigate the world without any family living nearby. Also, this meant no family gatherings for the holidays unless I flew to my sister's house to celebrate with her in-laws.

Over the years, I accumulated many 'mothers' who weren't mine by blood, but tried to spoil me as much as they could. And I let them!

Despite the odds, I overcame domestic violence, along with physical abuse, neglect, narcissistic parents, cultural differences, almost claiming bankruptcy, and nearly being homeless in California.

I overcame because I didn't have a choice. But I made sure to have fun while overcoming my trauma.

If you can't let yourself relax and laugh out loud with friends, then you are limiting your progress in life. It takes a balance of fun and play. It's the angels' way, and they encourage us to take a break now and then.

Many friends I've made feel like family to me, and I gained a lot of acquaintances over the years who brought smiles to my face.

While in Cincinnati after my internship, I was hired by Hamilton County Children Services for my first position in social work. Around that time, I met my husband through another social worker. She introduced us, and we became fast friends. Once my manager left, I followed as it had been three years.

Next, I focused on supporting homeless families and assisting women as they transitioned back into the community, helping them secure employment, transportation, and mental health care. I visited them once a week and got to know their lovely souls.

One client taught me the importance of never giving up. She relocated from Columbus to Cincinnati to escape her abuser, who tried to stab her in the heart. While he was in jail, she started over in a new city, leaving her adult children behind. She did everything with grace. When I heard she died from a heart attack just months after stabilizing her new life in the community, it hit me.

Perhaps when our life lessons are over, that's when we go home?

After that, I worked at a nursing home. It wasn't my first choice, but I felt I needed to work with this population, as I never had grandparents.

I was shocked. On my first day at the facility, during my lunch hour, I stared out the window that faced a brick wall while listening to the groans of the confused in the dementia unit, and a tear slipped down my face.

Forcing myself to stay for one year was an eye-opening lesson on life and death. Many rehabilitation residents would be sent to the hospital and never return. Meanwhile, I assisted 100 long-term care residents with any needs they had.

My most bizarre request was that of a resident in her 50s who was on suicide watch because her boyfriend, who lived at another facility, passed away.

It was my job to find his ashes, as he had no family for a burial. To my amazement, I located them through the coroner's office, who delivered them to the facility, and her heart was so relieved! She passed away a few months later, and her family buried her with his ashes in her coffin. Crazy how life works.

If you trace your life from the present to the past, you'll see the correlations and how everything we went through was relevant.

Once you connect the dots, answers come to you about why something happened that you didn't understand at the time. It helps to clarify our journey. What's the common denominator? Is this your passion? Can you see yourself doing this as a form of income?

I started my business with a program I created called 'Heal Your Heart ~ Attract Your Soulmate,' a life coaching package that included spiritual mentorship.

Then, I developed my confidence to provide positive Oracle Card Angel readings, which are messages from my clients' angels. My angels helped me in the beginning by letting me know when to stop shuffling the cards and revealing a beautiful message.

I organized events, became a vendor at various convention centers, and my energy burst with glowing confidence, especially when I added four levels of Healing Touch for Animals® education. It brought me so much joy and still does!

During this time, I worked full-time as a social worker and eventually transitioned to part-time work, taking on small jobs to make ends meet.

Now, I've built my clientele for Healing Touch for Animals® and do this full-time, along with readings and counseling sessions with the angels. It's been nine years of learning, providing lightworker services, and continually expanding my angel artwork, jewelry, soaps, and decoupage vases. I even wear an angel wing necklace that lets people know I'm open to talking to angels.

Whatever your passion is, don't give up. If you have that gut feeling this is your life purpose, keep pushing forward and ask God and his angels for guidance.

I believe in miracles because each one of us is a miracle in itself. This book has been a dream come true, and my guardian angel made it easy for me to decide which avenue or agency to go through: Manifest It! LLC was wonderful!

Keep your eyes open for divine interventions that will soon push you in the right direction to reach your goals, and may your vibration and bright light lead you to your destiny!

Love & Light,
Maureen

Learn more about how I can help you and your beloved pets at https://maureen-hollmeyer.com/

FOOTNOTES & RESOURCES

CHAPTER 1

1. https://www.traumainformedcare.chcs.org/what-is-trauma/

2. https://www.thenationalcouncil.org/wp-content/uploads/2022/08/Trauma-infographic.pdf

3. https://www.nationalchildrensalliance.org/media-room/national-statistics-on-child-abuse/

CHAPTER 2

4. https://www.psychologytoday.com/us/blog/the-empaths-survival-guide/201812/are-you-empath-take-the-self-assessment-test

5. https://pmc.ncbi.nlm.nih.gov/articles/PMC4266064/#:~:text=The%20rate%20of%20suicide%20in,the%20general%20population%20(3)

6. https://nebraskaexaminer.com/2024/11/11/military-veterans-are-disproportionately-affected-by-suicide-but-targeted-prevention-can-help/#:~:text=November%2011%2C%202024%205%3A00%20am&text=That%20means%20that%20each%20day,represented%20among%20this%20tragic%20trend.

7. https://www.psychologytoday.com/us/blog/happiness-is-state-mind/202204/mental-health-among-mental-health-practitioners

8. https://pubmed.ncbi.nlm.nih.gov/16081404/#:~:text=The%20results%20of%20a%20preliminary,of%20the%20working%20age%20population

9. https://www.techtarget.com/pharmalifesciences/news/366608093/Healthcare-Workers-Are-at-a-32-Greater-Risk-of-Suicide#:~:text=Compared%20to%20non%2Dhealthcare%20workers%2C%20registered%20nurses%20are%2064%25,social%20and%20behavioral%20health%20workers.

10. https://www.healthline.com/health/full-moon-effects

CHAPTER 3

11. https://www.angelmessenger.net/how-to-communicate-with-angels-practical-tips-and-techniques-for-connecting-with-the-divine/

12. Doreen Virtue - Angel Numbers 101 https://books.google.la/books?id=VubWMoeco1cC&printsec=frontcover#v=onepage&q&f=false

CHAPTER 4

13. https://www.medicalnewstoday.com/articles/98432#1

ADDITIONAL RESOURCES

https://intuitivejourney.com/the-four-primary-archangels/

https://www.centreofexcellence.com/angel-messenger-12-signs/#4

https://reikirays.com/wp-content/uploads/2014/09/Archangels-Crystals-Chakra-Cheat-Sheet.pdf

Brian McCullon - Angel meditations - https://www.brianmccullen.com/

https://www.learniet.com/

ABOUT THE AUTHOR

Maureen Hollmeyer's fascination with angels began at the age of nineteen when she realized her guardian angel had saved her life while white-water rafting. This personal experience ignited her passion for healing, which has become a central focus in her life's purpose.

Maureen is now the CEO of Angelic Guidance ~ Healing for You and Your Pet. She holds a bachelor's degree in Social Work and is a top-ranked, certified healer in the worldwide Healing Touch for Animals Program. Over the past twenty years, she has been a dedicated frontline social worker in the Cincinnati, Ohio, community, contributing several articles to *CincyPet Magazine* and *Infinity Health Magazine*, as well as to two best-selling spirituality books.

In her free time, Maureen enjoys making angel-themed jewelry and home decor, volunteering and fundraising, reading fiction novels, and swimming.

To learn more about how Maureen can help you and your pet heal from trauma and transition into a life of peace and fulfillment, please visit: https://www.maureen-hollmeyer.com

www.ingramcontent.com/pod-product-compliance
Lightning Source LLC
Chambersburg PA
CBHW070158100426
42743CB00013B/2962